HOAX

HOAX

A WOMAN'S JOURNEY TO REVEAL
THE INDOCTRINATION OF THE
JEHOVAH'S WITNESS CULT, ADDITION,
AND MENTAL HEALTH DIAGNOSES

PONY JEAN PARKER

W. Brand Publishing
NASHVILLE, TENNESSEE

j.brand@wbrandpub.com
W. Brand Publishing
www.wbrandpub.com

Cover design: Pony Jean Parker
Interior book design: designchik.net
Cover photo: Oscar Keys / Unsplash

Hoax —1st ed.

Available in Paperback, Kindle, and eBook formats.
Available in Hardcover, Paperback, Kindle, and eBook formats.

HC: 978-1-956906-43-1
PB: 978-1-956906-36-3
eBook: 978-1-956906-44-8
Library of Congress Control Number: 2022950774

Disclaimer from Author:
I am not a Mental Health Professional. The information contained in this book is not intended and should not be construed as medical advice or serve as a substitute for medical advice or diagnoses rendered to you by your individual doctor or other health care provider.

Note from Publisher:
Image size of backmatter History of Treatment is intentional.

CONTENTS

To those closest to me, without you, none of this,

my life, would be possible.

For David Leytus

"I think this man is suffering from memories."

– Sigmund Freud 1895

PART I

IN THE BEGINNING

April 21, 1982, Santa Monica California.

So here we were, a family of six: Dad, Mom, Brother, Sister, Brother and then me. My earliest memories were of sharing the second bedroom of that tiny home with all my siblings, how my eldest brother went to school and got chickenpox and my mom made us all take turns sharing a bed with him so we would all get it at the same time. How the dining room table was a rounded corner kitchen nook that I adored so much, even at that young of an age. Our backyard, if you could call it that, was a long skinny rectangle patch of grass enclosed by a tall white wooden fence.

I don't remember the age or time when I fully understood and comprehended I was born into and raised as one of Jehovah's Witnesses. It was a funny thing being immersed in something from birth. You had no other sense of reality and grew up believing that everything around you was normal and the only way to be. We all fell victim to that cult or not. *You are the product of your environment, right?*

Nature vs. Nurture—the age-old study and belief of how much either "nature" or "nurture" forms a person's characteristics. "Nature" means innate biological factors (namely genetics), while "nurture" can refer to upbringing or life experience. The CDC states that the **early years of a child's life are very important for later health and development.** One of the main reasons is how fast the brain grows, starting before birth and continuing into early childhood. Although the brain continues to develop and change into adulthood, the first eight years can build a foundation for future learning, health, and life success. Nurturing and responsive care for the child's body and mind is the key to supporting healthy brain development. Positive or negative experiences can add up to shape a child's development and can have lifelong effects. Nurturing a child by understanding their needs and responding sensitively helps to protect children's brains from stress. Speaking with children and exposing them to books, stories, and songs helps strengthen children's language and communication, which puts them on a path towards learning and succeeding in life.

My childhood was relatively normal and happy. Not to pass judgement or overrule anyone else's childhood experiences, but I think stating the ENTIRETY of my childhood was full of trauma and abuse would be a lie, but the things I endured didn't make it any less impactful as an adult. I loved school; I made friends easily. We moved a lot in the years I was five to ten years old. It felt like every six months we had to move to a new house.

My father was born and raised in the cult; my mother was "witnessed to" as a teen from a classmate in high school. It was my understanding we were the only ones who were worshipping God correctly. Everyone else in the world, anyone I met who wasn't a

Jehovah's Witness, was "Worldly" and a bad association. Basically, they were horrible people we could not be friends with. My classmates, horrible people. As a child, they taught us to label other children as evil and taught that since they are not also in the religion, they were not worthy of God's favor and would DIE and die soon. (If I had a dollar for every time over the years since they established this abusive cult that they proclaimed to know the year Armageddon would come, I would be a millionaire.)

Teaching your children from birth–from a young age of their very first developmental stage of brain development–to judge others severely and if the child didn't fall in line, they too would be killed. This indoctrination was child abuse. Born and raised this way, there was no level of comparison of what true reality and normalcy was. This was it. It engrained a thought process that we were doing the right thing and everyone else was wrong. I didn't know if it created the intended effect which was, feeling I was so different and special from the world in a good way, therefore gaining God's favor. In actuality, it led me to feel and believe that I was so different and weird. Also, I carried around this ideology that if I ever failed at anything, I would lose God's favor and be killed. At age five. The Organization was comfortable allowing a five-year-old to believe this.

They taught us to stand tall and defend our faith to others in school and even witness (witnessing is the act of sharing the propaganda of the religion to convince them to join the cult, same as door-to-door witnessing) to other children.

Growing up as a child in the late 1980s, we said the pledge of allegiance every morning in school, but that wasn't allowed in the cult. We had our own activities that revolved around every single holiday celebrated and recognized in this society, because we were not allowed to celebrate them.

It mortified me the first couple of days of each new school year when I would perform the pledge of allegiance. The idea of others seeing me *not* do it and asking me why or even teasing me or calling me weird for not doing so, I felt left out of all the activities and the joy of celebrating holidays in class. *Valentine's Day?* The kids had to be told to skip my desk and not involve me. *Thanksgiving?* Couldn't make a hand turkey. *Christmas?* Couldn't sing Christmas carols and make cotton ball snowmen.

I was allowed to be "friends" with classmates, but only in class. I had two childhood friends who were "worldly" that initially I was allowed to be friends with outside of school. I went to their houses, but I don't really remember them coming to mine. Because my friends had better snacks and board games about teen dating that I could never have at home, I really liked going to their homes. I was never allowed to spend the night, though; it was always explained to me I couldn't because they weren't Jehovah's Witnesses and therefore it was against the rules for me to do so. So, I could associate with them at school, hang out at their houses, but could never spend the night. *WHAT WAS HAPPENING?*

All this sounded frivolous, but as a child it was our existence of acceptance to our peers and a life lesson on how we were to feel and act at all times. They inundated us with the ideology that if we didn't fall in line with all of these things, God would KILL US.

I remember being at the meetings sometimes and the brother on the podium explained in his talk how we had to have a fear of Jehovah and I thought, *yes, I definitely have that, God is mean and I have to be perfect.* So now, I had the standard of wanting to make my parents happy and live up to their standards, and also, I had this overwhelming fear of a God up in heaven somewhere apparently who, to my understanding, was waiting for me to fail him and then he would kill me.

This created such an unhealthy idea of perfection I had to live up to, shame and guilt when I failed to do it perfectly. It taught me I had to be perfect, or I was unloved and deserving of death. Please read that again and let it sink in. Through the most pivotal stage of brain development, I was raised with the idea that if I was not perfect, I would lose the favor of my parents and a God in heaven would want me to die. *How did anyone in a high control religion feel this was OK to do to children?* A cult thrives on mind control and brainwashing to create an individual that is too scared to think on their own.

Steve Hassan, well-known author of *Combatting Mind Control,* shared this article on the Freedom of Mind Resource Center website. This article was written by Sam Fade, a pseudonym of an ex-member of the

Jehovah's Witness cult who has extensive experience studying abuse in children.

The ACE score test is a tally of exposure to different kinds of abuse, neglect and other childhood trauma or dysfunction. At the very least Jehovah's Witness children will ALWAYS score a 2 on the ACE test. Most, like me, scoring way higher due to strict corporal punishments, abusive parents, mental illness, sexual abuse etc. The two ACE components that Jehovah's Witness children are always subjected too, sometimes without parental knowledge, are emotional abuse and emotional neglect.

Emotional abuse comes in the form of severe indoctrination, restrictions of freedoms, constantly being in the flight or fight mode due to doomsday teachings, restrictions on freedom of identity and pressure to conform. Again, some of these deprivations of liberty go against the United Nations Charter on the rights of a child. These all add up to an emotionally abusive atmosphere.

Emotional neglect is the other ACE score witness children will always have. This is again due to severe adherence to doctrine to the detriment of a child's identity. Parents are focused on witnessing, meeting attendance, control and compliance of their child to do exactly what the rules of the organization state. This blind adherence fails children's emotional needs; it doesn't allow them to freely express themselves without fear of repercussion.

Young children under chronic stress often fail to develop those secure relationships with their caregivers and then do not have a basic sense of trust or security in the world. Jehovah's Witness children are under chronic stress at all stages of their childhood. One of the key doctrines of the religion is that of Armageddon. Magazines, books, their door-to-door preaching, online content and talks from the pulpit are all focused on the impending doom and mass genocide that is coming. Their literature is littered with pictures of this mass genocide. These pictures are confronting for adults and children. The organization places great importance on emphasizing that this impending doom is coming any day or right around the corner and to "live in expectation of it" these are all common phrases used in the literature, online videos and from congregation meetings.

During these five years I had a strange fixation with "injuries" by faking sickness, faking I hurt my foot, my arm, etc. I didn't know why, and I still don't. *Maybe for attention?* My mother was a stay-at-home mom mostly; my father worked in the auto industry, specifically auto body work and worked at a body shop in Santa Monica an hour away. We only saw him on weekends. By the time he got home from work in traffic we were already in bed and sometimes, but not too often, he wouldn't come home at all. He stayed in LA at my grandparent's, his parents' house.

But on the weekends, he would take us to our school to play on the field. We always played football. I was never a girly girl; I was always more of a tomboy.

Football became and still is one of my favorite things in this world.

The strangest part of it all (well, sadly this will not be the strangest part), was my father hardly ever attended any JW meetings, maybe a Sunday meeting, the Sunday session of a convention and/or the yearly memorial. Yet, we were overwhelmed with the responsibility of being a good JW and attend all meetings and go out in Field service. It seemed hypocritical to have one of my two primary sources of guidance literally demanding I fall in line while never doing it himself.

For as long as I could remember, I knew that my back was not OK. My parents used to tell me how they noticed that something was wrong when I was very young. Two bumps protruded from my chest on my sternum. They had three kids before me and none of them looked like this. Clearly, something was not right.

Kyphosis: an exaggerated curvature of the upper (thoracic) spine that creates a hunchback appearance. They estimate the prevalence of kyphosis to affect 4-8% of the general population and equally affects males and females, though this finding is debated in medical literature.

So here I was, hunchback (my childlike perception, of course) and in grade school, going to doctor's appointments here and there to assess my situation. My spinal curve was severe and my lumbar tilted backward, causing my pelvic bone to tilt as well. The options were easy, surgery consisting of putting a metal rod on each side of my spine (posterior spinal fusion with instrumentation) or wearing a full body brace at the beginning of puberty. I'm not sure if I was ever fully aware of or what all this meant. Maybe I blocked it all out.

I remember when my parents made the decision to try the brace, my father discussed how expensive it was. My whole life, I would never have insurance. This was in the 1990s when it was completely acceptable for insurance companies to reject coverage for "preexisting conditions". I understood it was a burden. I remember going to have the brace molded. They took a cast of my body from my navel to the tops of my legs. The brace would be made from this mold.

I was nine years old.

A Milwaukee Brace. An active corrective spinal orthosis. It consisted of a bar around my neck, one bar straight down the front, two bars down the back, and all three bars attached to a plastic girdle that was molded from my cast. I wore this 24/7, and only allowed to take it off to shower or swim in a pool; I even had to sleep with it on.

I felt different and ugly. Envious of the girls in my class who had pretty faces and magnificent hair with designer hairspray in their bathrooms, I would never be that girl. I was awkward, tomboyish, and had a metal bar around my neck. I was the weird Jehovah's Witness girl in class. From a young age, I embraced this and tried to make the best of it. Maybe it was my outstanding ability at nine years old to turn my trauma into humor. *Who knows?* I think it's true about trauma from childhood being character building. *What other choice did I have?* I could sink or swim.

With great sadness, I think about coming to terms with that at such a young age. In my family, I felt normal. I was inside the JW bubble. The point was made during these times that in the "New System of Things" I would be made perfect and all things wrong with me would go away. *Why couldn't they just go away now? Why did I have to wait till the end of this system of things and Armageddon to come?* It left me feeling like I wasn't good enough for God to fix. I was doing something wrong.

Living with this brace wasn't easy, although for the most part, kids didn't care; kids never saw the brace. Adults though, *phew.* People came up to my mom and literally said: "What's wrong with her?"

My mother came to my classroom in second grade and stood up in front of my class and gave a lesson on how people were different and how my brace didn't make me any different from them. *Dear God, why?* I knew her intention was to protect me, but the only comments I remembered were kids asking where the braces on my teeth were.

I wore this till I was almost fourteen, I felt I definitely had to try harder to be accepted and be "cool", to look more grown up or different or better. I tried to do my hair in a cute way or wear lipstick. I became the funny girl in school to distract, perhaps by creating a distraction from this monstrosity of metal around my body which made me look as if I had a disability.

When I was little, I was a big reader. I loved to read, former *Babysitters Club* member here. At the bookstore one day, I knew I was going to be able to pick out a new book. Growing up in the era of Judy Blume, I was led to see what books she had that I had never read before. I was attracted to this one book, *Deenie*; there was this beautiful girl on the cover with dark hair like mine. I read the description of the book: "When Deenie sees the brace for the first time, she wants to scream . . . is stuck wearing a brace from her neck to her hips for four years or longer."

Diving into this book, I learned this beautiful girl on the cover, an aspiring model, had a form of scoliosis that led her to have to wear a Milwaukee Brace. I couldn't believe it. I was a teenager in a Milwaukee Brace. I wanted to be a model. I, for once in this whole ordeal, felt like I wasn't alone.

Years later, as an adult, I wrote an email to Judy Blume thanking her for this story. She graciously responded to the email thanking me for sharing my story with her. It was purely random, or perhaps a divine intervention, that I came across it in the first place, but regardless, it was something that helped me make it through. I still have the same copy I bought when I was a child. I display it proudly in my bookcase.

Near the end of elementary school, we moved in with my fraternal grandparents for a short time. I later learned my father had to file for bankruptcy and build the family back up financially to afford our own place. My grandfather was an Elder of the congregation.

Wikipedia defines Jehovah's Witness Elders as:

Each congregation has a body of elders, who are responsible for congregational governance, pastoral work, selecting speakers and conducting meetings, directing the public preaching work and creating "judicial committees" to investigate and decide disciplinary action for cases that are seen to breach scriptural laws.

There are no secular educational requirements for elders; however, training programs are offered for elders within the organization. Elders are considered *"overseers"* based on the biblical Greek term, ἐπίσκοπος (episkopos, typically translated *"bishop"*). Prospective elders are recommended from among ministerial servants and former elders by the local elder body for appointment by the circuit overseer.

Particular roles within the body of elders include:
- Congregation Secretary: maintains congregation records, reports congregation activity to the branch office, advises the congregation about conventions and assemblies, and oversees those handling accounts
- Coordinator of the Body of Elders: chairs elders' meetings, assigns duties and speakers for most congregation meetings, and cares for certain financial matters
- Group Overseers: oversees groups for public preaching and pastoral care
- Life and Ministry Meeting Overseer: ensures that the Life and Ministry Meeting is handled according to the instructions set by the Watch Tower Society and schedules student assignments
- Watchtower Study Conductor: leads the weekly study of The Watchtower

- *Operating Committee Members: responsible for the care of the building and property of Kingdom Halls that are shared by two or more congregations*
- *Public Talk Coordinator: schedules speakers and talks for public meetings and co-ordinates traveling speakers from his congregation*
- *Service Overseer: organizes matters related to public preaching, and oversees those handling Witness literature and territories*

It was intimidating to be living under the roof of an Elder. I felt the need to be even MORE perfect than I was already trying to be. This man held authority that was "appointed by God" and if he found out I didn't believe (which was starting to happen) or that I acted in a way that was unfavorable to God, he would tell God and I would die. I felt a level of responsibility to be a perfect example because at this point my siblings and I were known as the grandchildren of one of the longstanding Elders of Los Angeles. All congregations in the area knew who he was, and I was terrified someone would tell on me if I did anything "wrong", and it would get back to him.

After almost a year of living there, we finally moved into our own home.

It was a typical house in Culver City, California built in 1940: big front porch, three bedrooms, one-and-a-half baths, detached garage in the back. The front of the house had a large window that the couch was placed in front of. I would sit there and watch TV or the street outside; it was a very busy street for cars. My sister and I shared a bedroom in the front of the house. The middle of the house was my parents' bedroom and then the back of the house was my brothers' bedroom. Living room, dining room, and kitchen. There was a corner built-in in the dining room I always adored; shelves with a cabinet on the bottom. My mother always displayed her mother's dishes there.

For the most part, my memories of this house were beautiful. I enjoyed many amazing times here, with family, with friends. I can still hear my mother in the kitchen early in the morning; she never tried to do anything quietly. I think she assumed we should all be up as early as her. The house always smelled so good. My mother was the embodiment of Martha Stewart, cooking, baking, gardening, crafts, etc., you name it; she does it or has done it. She would often have cinnamon and spices boiling on the stove in the winter or fresh flowers from her garden in the spring and summer for their pleasant aromas. Mashed potatoes were my favorite thing she made (her secret was putting cottage cheese in them).

The main bathroom vanity was made of seafoam green tile. It was so beautiful. It had one tiny window we would have to open when we showered to let the steam out so the walls wouldn't mold.

For years my father could always be found sitting at the dining room table after work; after dinner, he would work and drink Bacardi and coke. For most of my life, it felt like this was all he did. He worked hard and then worked again at home. He could never be bothered. My father had a very short temper, very intimidating. He spanked us with his belt for years.

One time my sister went to tell on me because she said I was "wearing her socks". My dad came into the room and hit me repeatedly, without warning. I was so hurt and confused. Later that day, he found me in my grandfather's study and apologized. He told me he was going to take me to get ice cream to make up for it. I was old enough and aware enough at that age to understand he was, in his own way, apologizing for hitting me for no reason. His favorite retort when heated was, "I'll give you something to cry about!".

Once I graduated from elementary school, they put me in home schooling. My parents did not feel comfortable with us going to public school; they said it was dangerous and the influence of worldly kids was harmful and unacceptable. My mom started working full time to help with bills, so they left me at home all day with my other siblings, stuck in the house all day long. I hated it so much. I loved people. I loved interacting with people. The only way I got that interaction was by going to the Kingdom Hall. I did horribly in school the first two years because I was so angry about being home schooled. I just didn't care. The Kingdom Hall and going to meetings became my only source of social interaction, but every congregation we were in never had any kids my age. My siblings had kids their ages to bond and hang out with. I was always two or three years younger than all of them.

Throughout my life, drinking was normalized, and I became aware of what being "drunk" meant early in life. For as long as I can remember, my dad had always been a drinker, not a drunk. That was my perception as a child into adulthood, anyway. I think I saw my dad drunk twice as an adult, visibly intoxicated that is, truth was he was drunk A LOT, and only because I was of age to understand what that was. He drank Coors out of the original gold can it used to come in back in the 80s. Occasionally, he would tell me to go get a Dixie cup from the bathroom (we used them to rinse our mouths out from brushing our teeth). He would then fill up that Dixie cup with beer and hand it to me. I am sure I didn't realize the full meaning and impact of doing this so young. I'm pretty sure I just thought it was cool. I was five years old.

My dad and his best friends were all drinkers. My dad would drink a fifth of Bacardi Rum every night after work. He started his own windshield repair business and again, he was gone all the time, left for work before we woke up, came home at 6pm or later and immediately sat at the kitchen table and continued to work or pay bills. I remember seeing my dad drunk on the weekends and he was so happy and laughing at everything. I didn't know that I fully connected at that point that he was intoxicated. The connection I made was alcohol made him happy and nice. My dad typically was a very stern, intimidating person who I was very scared of, and he thrived on that, so seeing him laughing and being silly and doing practical jokes was so awesome. I loved it. For those brief periods of time, I wasn't scared of him.

One day when I was twelve years old, my mother took my sister and one brother to their scheduled orthodontist appointment, leaving my eldest brother who was sixteen to watch over me. He told me that as soon as mom left, he wanted to talk to me about something and made it sound fun. I didn't remember the exact words but he alluded to something "exciting" so I waited in anticipation for them to leave so my brother could tell me.

After they left, my brother sat me down on the living room floor in front of the huge stereo my parents had; it was a radio, cassette tape, and record player. My mother listened to Elton John's *Yellow Brick Road* album while cleaning. I always loved that stereo.

We sat a lengthy distance apart, while he proceeded to play "I'll Make Love to You" by Boyz II Men on the stereo. I was really confused at this point. He asked me what I thought of the song, and I told him I liked it. (Everyone did; it was a #1 song for 1000 weeks.) Although I was too young to understand what it REALLY MEANT. He then asked me if I was curious about doing what they talked about in the song, and that he wanted to do that with me.

At this point, I panicked inside. I felt a rush of adrenaline. Terror. Fright. I kept thinking that I was alone with him in the house, and I did not know what he was going to do to me. I asked him if I could please go to my room, and he said OK. Going to my room, I shut the door, and sat on the corner of my bed furthest from the door.

A few minutes later, I heard a knock on my door. He opened it, stood in the doorway, and asked me not to tell anyone what had happened. I said OK, so he would leave my room since I was still scared of what he may do.

I waited for what seemed like forever for my mom and other siblings to return. My bedroom was in the front of the house and one window right next to my bed gave a perfect view of the street and driveway. I had a clear view when they arrived home. When they did, the first person I told was my sister. She immediately urged me to tell my mom. I was scared. My sister shared with me he had approached her recently and said that she should wear a suit (the garment males wore to the Kingdom Hall) and he would put on a dress of hers. She thought it was weird.

She physically went to get my mom and brought her into our bedroom so I could tell her. I told my mom exactly what happened. She asked me if he had touched me in any way and I said no because that was the truth. He hadn't. She quickly called my dad at work and told him to come home immediately. I was terrified. My father was a very intimidating man when I was a child. I was scared of him, for no reason other than he was big and had a big voice and yelled sometimes.

When my father came home, my mother told him what I had told her in front of me and my father stood there listening, looking a little lost. He eventually walked to the back of the house where the boys' room was. I could hear him yelling at my brother, though I could not make out the exact words. When it was over, my father came to my room and told me, "It was a misunderstanding" that I misunderstood what my brother was saying, and it didn't happen and that I was to tell no one about it and my mother was to never bring it up to me again either. *What was happening?* I sat there in confusion and disbelief.

I was twelve years old.

I was defenseless, having only my parents to rely on as any twelve-year-old should and I felt unprotected and like no one believed me. So, at twelve, I had to learn how to handle and deal with the constant thoughts going through my head all by myself. *Is it how I dressed? Talked? Walked? Something? that caused him to do this to me.*

My father agreed to let me go stay at my grandparent's house for a week. He would tell them the reason for my stay was they could use help watching me for the week. Under no circumstances was I allowed to tell them what happened.

I was so happy to leave. My grandmother was my favorite person, and I would be with her for an entire week. We made cookies. We made sun tea, watched *In the Heat of the Night*, one of her favorite shows, went to Burger King and had Whoppers, sat, and had hot tea every night while playing cards.

The worst part was when we went clothes shopping one day. We went to Ross; it was one of her favorite stores and the second I walked in I felt ill. It disturbed and bothered me so much; all I thought about was, *Is this why? Clothes? All I do is wear jeans and big t-shirts? I don't want to get any cute clothes. I don't want to look good. I don't want him to think I'm attractive.* Although she didn't know what had happened, I felt protected by her. I was already close with her, but I clung even tighter during these times.

That week could never have been long enough. That feeling of love and protection is something I still chase all these years later.

I returned home to such awkwardness. He didn't leave and having to live with him and see him every day knowing I KNEW WHAT HE DID, that he LIED about it, and my own PARENTS did not protect me, never got easier as the years went on, only more tolerable in a sick, twisted way. My feelings had to deaden.

In the morning after my parents had left, my brother would walk around the house in front of me with a full erection. I told no one because I didn't think they cared anyway. My brother eventually left when he was twenty-one and joined the military. At boot camp, the only communication option we had was to send letters. My father told all of us we had to write him a letter since he was out there all by himself.

I wrote him a letter, calling him out for what he did to me and how it made me feel, for being a liar, for making it so that dad called me a liar and for putting me through something so traumatic. He wrote back, acknowledging and taking responsibility for his actions and apologizing. I never told anyone in my family about that letter. They wouldn't have cared anyway. All this time, they stood in their version of events that it never happened, and I was a liar. For me, though, it helped me move on and that was all that mattered. I still have that letter to this day. I have never read it more than once.

At age twelve or thirteen, I started drinking. We went to Palm Springs all the time for a weekend or on the holidays (because everyone was off from work). My mother would rarely go because the excessive heat gave her migraines. So, my dad would go to the store and buy my sister and me wine coolers; good ole Bartels & Jaymes. I remember the sweet buzz of the alcohol (3.2% but hey, I was a young teenager), drinking them and being in the sun in Palm Springs. Having a low buzz and the warmth from the sun made it heavenly. I felt so relaxed, so carefree, so GROWN UP. It made me forget what was happening in my mind as well, a cure for all my anxieties and a shut off of my thinking. My father did it all the time, so what's the problem here? Yes, I wasn't of age and not even close, but I was doing it with my father and his supervision, so that fact didn't matter.

This continued all throughout my teenage years. It escalated to where we didn't have to be in Palm Springs to drink, if my best friend was over, he would go buy us wine coolers and bring them to our bedroom and always say, "Don't let your mom see this". Mom wasn't a drinker, a glass of chardonnay here and there randomly but it wasn't her thing. Also, we all knew if she found out about this, she would lose it.

In these moments, I felt connected with my dad; he was no longer scary. In these times as well, I would accompany him to late night diners where we would eat and talk, just the two of us. I think this was my subconscious way to gain his love and approval. His lack of protection traumatized me, so I threw myself into bonding with him and essentially "making him love me" because since that incident, I felt he didn't and probably never had.

I believe being the youngest of four provided me with the "opportunity" of growing up a little faster than my age. Along with this situation, I grew up way too fast. I gained a smart mouth that next year, as I guess any thirteen-year-old would. But I also formed a strong sense of independence, like I was the only one who could really look out for me. On top of that, my mother and I, who were close before, had become distant. I would constantly second guess her words and demands and overrule her in front of people as if I was the "authority" of the situation. I'm not sure if this had anything to do with being thirteen or because of the situation I went through. Maybe both.

Thinking about it now, I reacted opposite from my parents' lack of protection. With my dad, I fought for his acceptance; with my mother, I despised her for having it yet not protecting me.

During this time as well, I became so much more aware of the teachings and indoctrinations of the cult. Being that it was not allowed to question the rules and teachings, let alone act on engaging in one thing they were against, it left me feeling defective and broken. *Why was I questioning them? What was wrong with me?* If I didn't fall in line, God was going to kill me but, I couldn't shake the feeling or help feeling that I didn't agree or understand it.

These are the majority though not all of their rules and standards. Jehovah's Witnesses are not allowed to:

1. Belong to another organization or club for the purpose of socializing with nonbelievers
2. Have best friends and activity buddies who are not Jehovah's Witnesses
3. Associate with people outside their organization when it is not necessary
4. Attend social functions sponsored by their employer unless attendance is required
5. Associate with coworkers after business hours in a social setting
6. Disagree with their organization's rules and code of conduct
7. Disagree with their organization's doctrines
8. Contribute to the Presidential Campaign Fund on their tax return
9. Join the armed forces and defend their country
10. Say the Pledge of Allegiance
11. Salute the flag
12. Vote
13. Run for leadership in their organization (JW's are "appointed" and invited to be leaders.)
14. Run for leadership in any organization
15. Take a stand for any political issue inside their organization
16. Take a stand on any political or "worldly" issue outside of their organization
17. Campaign for a political candidate
18. Hold political office
19. Discuss politics

20. Be a union steward or shop steward
21. Actively be involved in a union strike
22. Use a gun for protection against humans
23. Become a police officer if a gun is required
24. Wear military uniforms or clothing associated with war
25. Take yoga classes and practice the discipline of yoga
26. Smoke tobacco and cigars
27. Work full time selling tobacco and cigars
28. Attend Alcoholics Anonymous
29. Donate blood
30. Have blood transfusions
31. Read books, magazines, publications, and literature from other religions
32. Buy anything from a church store
33. Buy something at a church garage sale
34. Donate items to a church run store
35. Shop at the Salvation Army
36. Work for the Salvation Army
37. Work for another church
38. Play competitive sports on a school team
39. Play competitive sports professionally
40. Run for class president
41. Become a cheerleader
42. Go to the school prom or school dance.
43. Attend class reunions
44. Be hypnotized
45. Accept Jesus as their mediator
46. Join the Boy Scouts
47. Join the Girl Guides

48. Join the YMCA
49. Serve on jury duty
50. Study psychology, philosophy, sociology, and viewpoints that might shake their faith
51. Attend other Christian churches
52. Attend nondenominational churches
53. Attend non-Christian churches
54. Get married in another church
55. Dating non-believers is discouraged
56. Casual dating is discouraged
57. Dating someone without the intent of getting married
58. Having sex before marriage
59. Breaking an engagement, separation, and "unscriptural" divorce may result in disciplinary action
60. Marriage to non-believers is not recommended
61. Be gay or lesbian. Homosexuality is not acceptable.
62. Throw rice at a wedding
63. Get divorced unless the reason is adultery
64. Can't remarry unless their ex commits fornication first
65. Toast drinks
66. Buy a raffle ticket
67. Play bingo
68. Gamble
69. Sing any holiday songs
70. Sing the National Anthem
71. Celebrate Christmas

72. Celebrate New Year's Eve
73. Celebrate Easter
74. Celebrate Mother's Day
75. Celebrate Father's Day
76. Celebrate birthdays
77. Celebrate Thanksgiving
78. Celebrate Flag Day
79. Celebrate Veteran's Day
80. Celebrate Independence Day
81. Celebrate Saint Patrick's Day
82. Celebrate Valentine's Day
83. Celebrate Halloween
84. Celebrate Hanukkah
85. Accept holiday gifts
86. Celebrate any holiday except the death of Jesus
87. Partake in the bread and wine that represents Christ unless they are part of the 144,000
88. Make holiday artwork for school
89. Engage in holiday parties at school
90. Take on a leadership role in school
91. Porneia
92. Do suggestive and immodest dancing in a public place
93. Attend a class, workshop, or seminar, sponsored by another church
94. Attend social events or fund raisers sponsored by another church
95. Use of bad language (curse words) is discouraged
96. Wear blue jeans, shorts, and overly casual clothing at the Kingdom Hall. *See Dress Code.*

97. Wear pants at a Kingdom Hall if you're a woman
98. Wear revealing clothes or skirts that are too short (looked down upon)
99. Wear long hair or facial hair if you're a man (depends on the local customs of the country you live in)
100. Body piercings are discouraged
101. Tattoos are discouraged
102. State or imply that the Watchtower is not run by Jehovah God
103. Have discussions and express Bible based viewpoints that contradict the organization's beliefs
104. Say anything negative about their organization. JW's must "speak in agreement" and be "like-minded"
105. Consider other religious beliefs as valid and truthful.
106. Acknowledge any prayer spoken by a non-believer as valid
107. Take another Jehovah's Witness to court (with exceptions)
108. Wear or own a cross
109. Own any religious picture
110. Own any religious statue
111. Engage in idolatry
112. Believe in miracles (except those found in the Bible)
113. Believe in ghosts
114. Witchcraft

115. Black magic
116. White magic
117. Consult with a psychic or become one
118. Study tarot cards, get a reading or give a reading
119. Study numerology or get a reading
120. Dabble in ESP (extrasensory perception), dowsing, or divination
121. Use a tool such as a pendulum to access information from the spiritual realm
122. Attempt to communicate with departed spirits
123. Attend a seance
124. Believe in good luck or say things such as "Good luck to you"
125. Believe or say anything superstitious
126. Prophesy
127. Speaking in tongues
128. Laying on of hands
129. Energy healing such as Reiki
130. Read their horoscope
131. Study astrology or zodiac signs
132. Combat training, boxing, or martial arts
133. Go to heaven unless they are part of the 144,000
134. Worship Jesus as God
135. Idolize any celebrity or love and admire them to excess
136. Women can't be elders
137. Women can't be ministerial servants (assistants to the elders)

138. Divulge secret information to enemies and
     those not entitled to know
139. Greet or talk with disfellowshipped persons
     (with some exceptions)
140. Associate with disfellowshipped persons ex-
     cept for immediate family living in the same
     house
141. Keep secrets from the organization. Jehovah's
     Witnesses report friends and family mem-
     bers breaking the rules

The biggest of them all was that I was to believe
that I wanted to be part of a belief from such a hateful God. His "truth" had left me unprotected from so
many things I should have never endured. There were
so many contradictions. The main one as a young teenager was: "How are we expected to witness to others
to bring them in to the religion if we are taught so continuously that anyone outside of this religion is evil and
we are not supposed to associate with them?"

The pressure put on me from not only myself but
from the perspective of everyone around me in the
congregation and my family to fall in line in a certain
way was overwhelming. I acted one way on the outside
for show and acceptance, but on the inside, it switched
back and forth continuously between terror of actually
thinking and feeling different, to wishing I could act
and feel different outwardly and be accepted.

They forced me to believe that these teachings were true:

a. Jehovah's Witnesses truly believe that they are the one and only true religion and that their leaders are directly appointed by God and should be obeyed as such. Jehovah's Witnesses believe that rejecting the teachings or instructions of the leaders means to reject God himself.

b. Jehovah's Witnesses also believe that Armageddon is coming very soon. In fact, many statements imply that this is going to happen in months, not years. When this day comes, Jehovah's Witnesses believe (and teach) that those who are not baptized Jehovah's Witnesses will be killed. This includes their children and babies.

c. While many outside are well aware of the Jehovah's Witnesses' beliefs on blood transfusions, most are unaware that this is not a matter of "personal choice". Jehovah's Witnesses believe that to accept a blood transfusion means to be cast off by God and killed at Armageddon. In the meantime, the offender must be expelled and subsequently shunned by their friends and family.

d. This brings us to the Jehovah's Witnesses' beliefs on disfellowshipping. Jehovah's Witnesses believe that a disfellowshipped person has been rejected by God and will be executed at Armageddon. They also believe that they are required to cut off all contact with the disfellowshipped individual, even if that person is a close relative. This includes mothers, fathers, sons, and daughters. Jehovah's Witnesses believe that "strict avoidance is really necessary".

e. Lastly, Jehovah's Witnesses believe that holidays such as Christmas, Easter, Halloween, and birthdays are pagan and constitute Apostasy and the celebration of false religion. This includes putting up a Christmas tree, saying "cheers", making a toast, and even saying "bless you" when someone sneezes! Offenders will be disfellowshipped if they fail to be sufficiently repentant.

Being older and having the cognitive ability to comprehend these things may have been even worse than what they indoctrinated in me as a child. What a thought to have to think about which mental trauma was worse than the other.

Then I started rebelling. I was always the more "rebellious" one out of all of us, anyway. I wore clothes and makeup I wasn't supposed to, listened to music I wasn't supposed to, talk to boys on the phone I wasn't supposed to; I didn't have a care in the world.

My first real boyfriend and first kiss was with a boy three years older than me. I was thirteen; he was sixteen. I was so enamored with him. We made excuses to talk to each other at the Kingdom Hall. The people in the congregation always had gatherings and we would always find a way to talk the whole time. My sister and I went to his house with other friends and hung out. We waited for our parents to go to bed and then we would sit and talk on the phone until 2 or 3am or one of us fell asleep. I'd never forget the first time he kissed me; I felt this jolt of electricity through my body, adrenaline, that lasted for HOURS. It was then, for the first time, I felt a hard penis.

I was the pretty sister who garnered the attention of boys. It was amazing until, shortly after the electricity faded, this boy would change his mind and want to be my sister's boyfriend. This continued off and on until I was fifteen. He liked me; he liked my sister back and forth and back and forth. His mother despised me; she thought I was "wild". My sister, on the other hand, was a saint and "so ideal".

I became obsessed with looking sexy and being all I could be for a male to want to give me attention. Hyper-sexuality set in, and I did everything to get away with it without my parents finding out or realizing. I loved the attention from boys and sadly, out in public, I would garner inappropriate attention from grown men, not realizing what that actually meant. To me it meant, "Oh wow they think I'm an adult. I'm so cool." I don't think I need to explain the level of messed up it is that I had resorted to this way of thinking.

My defense mechanism brought on by the things I'd been through and the lack of protection from my parents made me believe I was on my own and had to grow up and be older. Maybe I developed a complex that all I was worth was being sexual to someone. Maybe I hated myself and my parents so much I just didn't care. It might have been all of it, and more reasons I haven't uncovered yet.

Sexuality was always portrayed as unclean within the cult unless you were married and engaging in sex for procreation. Consequently, they looked down on pleasure with any sexual act. As a teen struggling to navigate hormones and emotions, it created another layer of disfunction and disappointment since having these thoughts and desires meant I was failing God and once again, worthy of death.

I was definitely rebelling in the sense of sneaking around and kissing boys. A part of me just wanted to be a normal teenager, and I was attracted to boys. There was nothing wrong with this progression as it was natural for a pubescent teenager to notice these things and feel emotions around it, but they taught us it was wrong.

"Jehovah's Witnesses are especially strict when it comes to sex and dating. Dating is only allowed with the intention to get married and only allowed when the person is of legal age, referred to by Jehovah's Witnesses as the "bloom of youth."

Even as adults, Jehovah's Witnesses couples who are dating are forbidden from being alone and require a chaperone at all times, even in public. Homosexuality is forbidden and is subject to severe punishment. But that's not even the tip of the iceberg. Here is a brief list of things Jehovah's Witnesses are not allowed to do when it comes to sex and dating:

- *Spend the night in the same house with a person of the opposite sex or a known homosexual if the person is of the same sex*
- *Masturbate*

- *Engage in "Passion-arousing heavy petting or caressing of breasts" out of wedlock*
- *Date anyone other than another Jehovah's Witness*
- *Go on a date without the supervision of a reputable chaperone*
- *Breaking off an engagement without a good reason to do so*
- *Separate or divorce, unless there is proven adultery*
- *Engage in any homosexual activity or accept the homosexual behavior of others*

Self-control (pertaining to thoughts of sex) is maintained by keeping up a good routine of Bible reading and study along with prayer. Usually when a person has a problem with constant improper thoughts, it's because that routine is lacking."

OK so, NOW I'm defective because I'm not reading the Bible enough? I read that damn thing all the time. I don't get it.

Around this time, I discovered I was attracted to females as well, and that was always portrayed as a sin as great as murder. Growing up in the 80s and 90s and having a front-row seat to the AIDS epidemic, they always taught me, as I'm sure society did as well, that being homosexual meant you were dirty and diseased, and you would die. *OK GOD, why did I think women were attractive? Was this a sick joke, another test of my faith and obedience to you?* I couldn't help being attracted to them and when the thought of it entered my mind, I felt nothing but shame and guilt and felt like something was innately wrong with me.

"Do not be misled. Those who are sexually immoral, idolaters, adulterers, men who submit to homosexual acts, men who practice homosexuality, thieves, greedy people, drunkards, revilers, and extortioners will not inherit God's Kingdom."—1 Corinthians 6:9, 10 – NWT

Excerpts directly from JW.org:

"Paul specifically mentioned those who evidently take on a passive sexual role and those who assume a more active 'male' role in their immoral relations. Thus, he made it plain that God disapproves of all homosexual acts."

"He condemned homosexual practices as unnatural and 'obscene.'"

"Although to some, the Bible's teachings may seem hard to follow, they are always 'healthful teachings,' that is, beneficial to the mind and the body. Homosexuality, on the other hand, can only be detrimental to one's physical, emotional, and spiritual well-being."

"Much homosexual sex is gruesome, violent, and downright sadistic."

"The homosexual life-style is marked by promiscuity, emotional distress, and disease."

The first time I got drunk, I was sixteen years old. My Dad was going out to dinner with his best friend and his wife to a restaurant on Rodeo Drive. I asked if I could go. I loved going out to eat with my dad. I felt like a grownup. When we got to the restaurant, my dad and his best friend sat at the bar, his best friend's wife and I sat at a table in the bar area. "Ask for a water," she said. I was like OK; I'll have a water. She ordered a lemon drop martini. They brought it to our table, one in a martini glass and another one still in the shaker. She told me to drink my water so she could pour the martini from the shaker into my glass.

You bet your ass I drank that water as fast as I could. Here I was on a late Saturday night, on Rodeo Drive in Beverly Hills, drinking lemon drop martinis at sixteen years old. I had my first one and got up the nerve to tell her about my brother asking me to have sex with him when I was twelve; I told no one before. I never talked about it before the warmth of a slight buzz made the words easier to flow. She listened and told me she was sorry I experienced that. I believe I shared many secrets with her that night. She was like a really cool aunt; she was easy to talk to. Three martinis later, I swayed as I walked and my dad, his best friend, and his wife looked at me like, "Oh shit what did we do?"

I became really good friends with a girl in Orange County. She was the niece of one of my uncles by marriage (my dad's sister was married to her dad's brother). From ages fifteen to eighteen, I felt I was living the best time of my life. I was into the punk rock scene of the late 90s in Orange County, wearing dickies, baby tees and all stars, hanging out with skater guys, going to Disneyland every Friday night with all our friends. It was amazing. Staying with her and her family, I had so much more freedom. We went out with our friends and came home at midnight, watched rated-R movies, and listened to whatever music we wanted. We went to house parties. With her, I went to my very first concert, behind my parents' backs.

Her parents always felt my dad was a little too strict and said since I was staying at their house, I would have to live by the rules they had there. They wouldn't tell my parents anything, but if my parents called and asked, they wouldn't lie (my parents NEVER CALLED to check on me). It was amazing. This fueled my addiction to living a double life and it being "acceptable".

Anyone who was a JW in their teens knew there was always a party to go to that stood for everything the cult was against. Underage drinking, people making out, listening to unapproved music, etc. I could finally express myself somewhat, to an extent where it was acceptable.

With that little taste of freedom of expression, I became the leader of bad influence; constantly testing the waters of those around me, seeing what was acceptable and what wasn't. I snuck into my friend's backyard in the middle of the night after her parents went to bed to make out with Witness boys. I wanted acceptance; I wanted to be the desirable one. Looking back, I realized I garnered the reputation of the girl that would "hook up".

Four months after I turned seventeen, I met my first husband at a Jehovah's Witness Convention. He was in the lobby with his friend. They came up to me because he thought I was pretty and wanted to talk to me. We fell fast and hard for each other. My parents had no idea I had a boyfriend. We hung out every time I was in Orange County. He had a car and my best friend and I didn't. We went to punk shows, hung out with his friends, did whatever we wanted. I smoked my first cigarette at that time.

Eventually my parents found out I had a boyfriend, and he came over a few times to meet them and hang out, etc. Everything was restricted, 9pm curfew. We could go out to eat or hang out at the house. I grew tired of it.

I pushed the boundaries of what was allowed. We would sneak off to parks alone in his car and basically do everything except have sex. He came to my work, and we would do those things there as well. We felt so in love we rented a hotel room, and both had sex for the first time.

We continued to do this for months. My best friend would lie and say I was with her and really, I was in a hotel room somewhere with him. Things escalated and our parents became stricter with us. He was baptized; I wasn't. His Dad was an elder, so there was more expected from him and whom he chose to date. His Mother hated me and hated the idea of us, even going as far as banning him from communicating with me or seeing me. We did anyway. As a teen, I think someone telling you no was just more fuel on the fire to doing the forbidden act anyway.

We came up with a plan to move me out of my home and get a studio apartment (in this case a converted garage with a room and bathroom and no kitchen) so we could move forward with our lives, dating and being adults making all our own decisions. One day while my parents were at work, I packed all my stuff into garbage bags; he picked me up, and I moved out.

Although I had memories of joy to look back on, I did all my middle school and high school classes in this home and learned dance moves to music videos with my cousin in the living room. We had the other teenagers and kids over to the house from our congregation and played dominoes and card games. This home felt like a safety net as much as it felt like a prison.

When they eventually figured it out after coming home from work that day, my father called and begged me to come home and I said no. He said if I came back, we could find a place in LA where I could live outside of their house. I never believed that for five seconds. He also said my actions were hurting my mother so much I had to come back. *What a horrible card to play! What about my feelings when your son wanted to rape me, and you defended him and told me I was a liar?*

I was sick of all the restrictions; I didn't say this to him, but I had grown such an independent spirit I felt I didn't need my parents. They were never there when I needed them anyway, and I felt like I was a true adult. Eventually, my best friend became jealous of my relationship and decided she was going to tell the elders of the congregation and my parents that I had been having sex.

Because of this and the backlash we did not want to receive, we ran off and eloped in Palm Springs, California. I was eighteen, and he was nineteen, turning twenty in October. I had graduated from high school two weeks before we got married. All that mattered to me was that everyone was going to leave us alone now; I was married, had my own life and was in charge of me.

PART II

SEX, GOD, AND ALCOHOL

What happened next was a very rude awakening.

I was so unprepared for the real world. My parents kept me so sheltered I was completely unaware of how to function as an independent adult. Although I had grown to be very independent emotionally, I was still completely dependent on them to survive.

My now husband and I were free to do and act however we wanted. We would go out all night and enjoy being young, smoking cigarettes, and going to punk shows. However, every time arriving home, I couldn't help but feel completely overwhelmed with feelings of guilt and shame for enjoying myself. *Why?* I was spending money left and right because I did not know how to budget.

We spent some nights buying food at the gas station just to have a meal because my dad gave me a gas card I could use. My husband and I both had to find new jobs because I had moved a sizeable distance from my previous job, and he worked for his parents at the time and his parents wouldn't allow him to work for them anymore since he married me.

Things weren't great. We had our issues. I tried to fool myself with the fact that I could now do whatever I wanted, and it was what I wanted, but all the while, still going to meetings and pretending because my husband was currently disfellowshipped. He was going through the motions of trying to get reinstated because again, that was the right thing to do.

There were moments of frustration and sadness at losing parts of our families because of this. It caused a lot of tension between us. My husband wanted a child so badly, he felt it was the next step and answer to everything. I never pictured myself having children, but I wanted to make my husband happy, so two months after we married, we tried to get pregnant.

We took a trip one night to Knott's Berry Farm, a theme park in Southern California, since rollercoasters have always been one of my favorite things. Was it the thrill of the motion of the ride or the feeling of danger? Maybe it was the moment of escape. It was probably all those reasons and more. In the car on the way home, I felt so nauseous and sick. The next morning, I took a pregnancy test, and it was positive.

I was excited that it made my husband happy, and I was fulfilling my role in life that I had always been told was meant to be, married at eighteen and starting a family. Sustaining a job was difficult for me. I suffered from extreme morning sickness. Our ability to keep our heads above water financially diminished. I called my dad one day and asked if we could come and live with them: "Dad, I want to come home."

We moved back in with my parents to get on our feet and have a softer landing now that I was pregnant. Since we were living in my parents' house, it was "OK" for my parents and one of my brothers to associate with my husband.

I'll never forget my first experience with true shunning. We had gone to Disneyland as part of my parents' anniversary celebration. This was a yearly occurrence. My husband and I showed up and one of my cousins were there. It was an immediate awkward, "Do I talk to you? Do I not talk to you? What do I do?" kind of moment. My cousin had the attitude of "I don't care," and we all hung out.

We had so much fun that night. My siblings, my husband, and my cousins, who I had always been super close to. Toward the end of the night, we met up with my parents, my aunt and uncle, and my dad's best friends who were back at the hotel. I remember walking up to them and all their faces fell and looked very stoic and serious. They treated my husband and me with hushed silences and looks of extreme judgement.

Later the next day, both my parents and my aunt told me the fact that we hung out with my cousins was inappropriate, since my husband was disfellowshipped. I could comprehend why because I knew the "rules" of the organization, but at the same time I was confused how their love could be so conditional. It only further pushed me to feel like an outsider and unaccepted by my family.

Staying with my parents was short-lived. My father was a controlling cruel man, something I knew very well, being raised by him. After they reinstated my husband, we moved in with his parents. Once that happened, it was like everything was fine. We were completely accepted and now the focus was on me having a personal study with a sister in the Kingdom Hall so I could get baptized.

Again, I fell in line as I knew what they expected me to do, and this was how I was supposed to live my life. I had a tiny ounce of freedom from the cult and being myself, but I soon returned to the indoctrination and mind control of how I was supposed to be and live my life. Sacrificing my own internal thoughts and feelings yet again to be accepted and loved by my family and those I loved. If I did these things, they would love me and want me. Also, if I didn't do this, I would die a horrible death in Armageddon and never live in paradise with my family. *Who wants that?*

Our son was born on April 11, 2001. I went into the hospital at 7am and had him by 1:30pm. He was the perfect little Gerber-looking baby with white-blonde hair. I did not know what I was doing other than fulfilling my duty as a wife and doing what my husband wanted. In my mind, that told me our marriage was good, and this would make it great.

The first six months, we lived with my husband's parents. This proved to be very difficult. My mother-in-law constantly referred to my son as "her baby" and made comments that if her tubes had not been tied, she would have another child. Mind you, while I was pregnant, she would also touch my belly and call it her baby and became so unsettled with the idea of being a grandmother, she wore an all-spandex jumpsuit to the baby shower she threw for us.

To be honest, I was not very good with motherhood the first year. I didn't truly enjoy it or bond with my son as I probably should have. I loved my son with all my heart, but it wasn't what I wanted, it was what my husband wanted. I was nineteen years old and wanted to be a nineteen-year-old. I wasn't working at the time. I was a full-time mom, and my husband was working and would come home and had very little involvement with taking care of our son because "he had worked all day". I grew to resent him and, in a way, resent my child. There were many times I would leave my son crying because I just didn't want to deal with him.

Then my worst nightmare happened; my grand-mother died.

I know grandmothers die every day, but to me I lost the only person I felt really loved me no matter who I was. The woman who, when I was sexually abused by my brother, took me in and cared for me even though she didn't know what had happened. She was my safe haven. She was the only reason why I was still loved in this family. To this day, thinking of her death still brings me to tears and makes me wish she was still here.

My grandfather gifted me her original high school portrait that I proudly have framed and displayed in my room next to the dried rose petals from a rose that had been on top of her casket at her viewing. A part of me was determined to continue being a Jehovah's Witness so that I would make it to paradise just to be with her again. The Jehovah's Witness Organization believes that after Armageddon, those who proved faithful to God will live forever on earth in paradise where there will be no more pain or sickness and we will all have wild animals as friends; damnit I wanted to be there with my grandmother and my pet lion.

Life moved on and as my son got a little older, I finally returned to working. One day my husband picked me up from work and on the way home said his mother mentioned to him I was not caring for the baby as I should and probably shouldn't be a mother anymore. She offered to raise our son along with my husband and I could just leave. This was no longer a conducive situation since my mother-in-law was trying to take over in such an inappropriate manner, regardless of my inability to truly bond with my son, his necessary needs were taken care of. I truly believed this resulted from me not getting baptized as quickly as they wanted and resulted in the decision, "OK we will just get rid of her". We soon moved out into our own apartment.

I quickly learned that my relationship with my husband was not all as it appeared. We got married ten months after we met, and our dating life was such a whirlwind of love. He was everything I wanted in a man, and he also fed my desire to be independent and free from limitations of the cult. As soon as we got married, the façade ended, and he showed his true colors as a narcissist. Throwing a newborn into the mix made nothing easier. After moving out, I really took to motherhood and bonding with my son. I was the primary caretaker; his dad was the fun parent without responsibilities.

My husband constantly lied about anything and everything he could. Even if telling the truth wouldn't get him in trouble, he would still lie. Never wanting to do anything one-on-one with me, he never paid attention to me unless he wanted sex. He was always with his brother and cousins and guy friends. The only time we ever went "out" was if we were going to meet up with his friends. He would lie about paying the bills. He would lie about spending money. He would lie about paying the babysitter. And he would lie about why he couldn't hold a job. When I would get upset, he would tell me, "It's because we don't have sex enough. That's why we have these problems". All our problems revolved around being sexual.

I worked a full-time job as the breadwinner of the family, and he worked part time. On his days off, he hung out all day with his best friend. I would come home and find porno movies shoved under the couch. *Are you really watching porn with your friend while taking care of our son?* That was the answer to everything, sex, until the answer became, he wanted another baby and that would make him so happy. All I wanted was to have my marriage, a *good* marriage and a good life. So, we began trying for another child because, THIS WOULD FIX EVERYTHING.

I found out I was pregnant the day after I turned twenty-one. We didn't tell anyone except for my sister initially. About two months into the pregnancy, I was at work and started bleeding heavily. I feared I had lost the baby. The doctor told me to stay off my feet for the rest of the weekend and on Monday go see my regular OB/GYN.

On Monday, the doctor told me it was so early in the pregnancy that it wouldn't show on the ultrasound. So, they had to do blood tests two days apart to see if my hormone levels were rising or falling. I would not know for six days whether this pregnancy had ended; six days I had to wait to see if I had lost my baby. At the end of it all, I didn't. My pregnancy attached very low, and I was not allowed to lift over five pounds, which proved to be very difficult, having a two-year-old at the time.

Things got worse instead of better with my husband. We grew apart; we fought all the time, so we decided to separate. I was four months pregnant and went to live with my parents. I saw my son every other week since my parents lived forty miles away from my husband, where he was living with his parents.

One evening, I had intense pain that felt like labor, and I asked my parents to take me to the hospital. I was only five months pregnant and was afraid I was losing the baby. They hooked me up to a monitor and told me I wasn't even contracting. I remember looking the doctor dead in the eye and telling him something was wrong. I had developed kidney stones. Because of the pregnancy, there was nothing they could do for me, and I just had to pass them.

My doctor was extremely uncomfortable with the fact that I lived forty minutes away and could not be present for emergency issues. I moved in with my sister near where my husband was so my doctor could treat me. Shortly after that, I went on bed rest for the duration of the pregnancy. I took medication every four hours to stop my body from contracting.

On November 18, 2003, I called my husband and asked him to come take me to the hospital because I could tell something was not OK. When we arrived at the hospital, it was determined I was in labor. There was only one other drug they could administer to stop the labor that was stronger than the one I was already on, and I would have to be admitted since it was through an IV infusion. They administered the drug. I fell unconscious, and my blood pressure fell to 70/50. They immediately took me off the medication and told me as long as the baby was not in distress, they would let me labor as long as possible.

My daughter was not due until January 1, 2004. They started injecting me with steroids to help develop her lungs and gave me an epidural to ease the distress on my body. Even though we were separated, I asked my husband to stay with me because, obviously, I was scared and worried. His reply was, "It's not comfortable for me to sleep here, so I am going to go home." My sister came and stayed with me the second night.

On the evening of November 20, 2003, the doctor assured everyone nothing was going to happen, so they all went home and left me at the hospital alone. I had not slept in two days. I was exhausted. The nurse came into my room and checked me without me waking up, then yelled at me to wake up so we could go to delivery. "I can see the baby's head . . . did you not feel that?!" I immediately burst into tears. Since I had an epidural, I felt nothing.

They took me to the delivery room. One nurse gave me her cell phone and I attempted to call anyone I could. My husband, my sister, my mom, were all nearby, but no one was answering their phones since it was after 10pm at night. I gave birth to my daughter with my doctor, two nurses, and two NICU nurses. They laid her on my chest for one minute and then immediately took her to the NICU unit. The next time I saw my daughter was the next morning, and she was on a ventilator.

I sat in a wheelchair and the doctor explained to me that her lungs were not strong enough for her to breathe on her own; she looked so tiny and helpless. I didn't know what to think or feel. Her condition stayed the same throughout that day. The next day they released me from the hospital. I went home to take a shower and come back to the NICU unit.

When I returned, I was told that she was not doing well. Her body wasn't oxygenating well enough to produce new blood. In delivery, I had transferred antibodies into her system that were killing off her blood supply; she was suffocating.

I stood there in a fog, like the world was moving around me and I was standing still. At that time, the doctors decided she needed a blood transfusion, something that is banned as Jehovah's Witnesses to accept and receive.

"Both the Old and New Testaments clearly command us to abstain from blood. Also, God views blood as representing life. So we avoid taking blood not only in obedience to God but also out of respect for him as the Giver of life."

A medical journal published by a pediatric nurse in 2005 stated: "Although there are no officially published statistics, they estimated that about 1,000 Jehovah Witnesses die each year through abstaining from blood transfusions."

I knew what I had to do. I had to reject the transfusion because all our families were there looking at us to do so. Is that what I wanted to say? Absolutely not. I wanted my daughter to live. *How could a God almighty want you to refuse such a lifesaving procedure? How was He OK with this?*

Before officially stating our refusal, the doctor informed me that if we refused, they would draw a court order to take custody of the child to force the transfusion, and she would remain in custody until they completed the procedure. That was my golden ticket to being able to say no. I knew no matter what, she would still get it and she would live.

We officially rejected the blood transfusion. There was a member of the hospital liaison committee with us in the hospital (the network within the Jehovah's Witness Organization providing authoritative information in regard to clinical strategies to avoid blood transfusion). After we received news that the transfusion had begun, he said, "Don't feel bad. This is saving her life." *WHY WOULD I?* Though this seemed simple and comforting, they used this tactic to make us think we SHOULD feel guilty.

Quickly after this statement, what followed was to pray to Jehovah and read the Bible more to gain forgiveness for the severity of what happened because it was such a huge sin. In addition, because the court order needed to be issued, they charged us with child abuse severe neglect for refusing the blood transfusion. We had to be interviewed downtown at the department's main office and have a home visit to check on our other child.

She spent seventeen days in the NICU unit. My mother and I were there every day from 9am to 6pm. The nurses said to me, "What are you doing here? You just had a baby go home and rest," and I would say to them, "My baby is HERE, and this is where I am going to be".

Friends and family visited over those seventeen days and her father–my husband–only visited once. Every time I called him, he had a different excuse. He even called me one time and asked me to see if my sister could babysit our son so he and his friend could go fishing.

In the middle of these seventeen days, I met with social services because our son tested for autism. It was determined that he had high functioning autism, a form of Asperger's and he needed to start therapy. So, I had a newborn fighting for her life and a child in need of intense therapy to help him. It overwhelmed me to do it all alone.

I would be lying if I said that I didn't think these scenarios I faced were all a result of my mind and heart not aligning with Jehovah's Kingdom. Honestly, up to this point every bad thing that had happened to me including the sexual assault by my brother, my failing marriage, and this blood transfusion weighed and tormented my mind to the point I believed these horrible things happened to me because I didn't love and believe in Jehovah like I should. *What God IS THIS?!*

Once my daughter was released from the hospital, I decided to get back together with my husband to see if we could make our marriage work. Now we had two kids, and I still chased the belief that I needed to fall in line and do what the Organization and my family expected of me. We lived with his parents. All four of us in one room.

I took our son to therapy three times a week with our newborn, and my husband worked. This lasted for six months before I realized nothing with him was ever going to change, lie after lie after lie.

Constantly putting his friends in front of me, we were like roommates, and I was so angry with him. Everything boiled down to his belief of, "if you had more sex with me then we wouldn't have any problems". He asked for two children, and I gave him exactly what he asked for. I took care of them. I fulfilled my role as a good Christian wife in the eyes of the congregation and did what they expected of me and yet, it was never, ever, ever going to be enough. He constantly held sexual acts and relations over my head to punish me and made me feel as if I was insufficient and defective in my role. I hated him. I resented him with every ounce of my being. I felt deceived, and I now had a life I never wanted to begin with.

I started spending a lot of time with family. We only have one girl cousin, and she is eight years younger than me. I would go to their house any chance I could get. It was my way of having fun. My sister and I and the kids would go.

It was there that I met Adam.

Adam was a friend of my family whom they met when they moved to Murrieta from Palm Springs. He was eighteen; I was twenty-two. He had my attention right away, and he knew it. It wasn't long before we exchanged numbers and texted each other here and there, initially nothing inappropriate and not very often.

Having the attention of an attractive male who thought I was witty, interesting, and attractive was wonderful. Our texts became more frequent, and we flirted in ways that could be excused as misinterpreted if seen by another. After all, I was married. This new-found interest gave me the courage to leave my husband. Our interest in each other grew and grew and we were at the point of obvious flirting in text messages. Someone wanted to be around me, and I felt loved. I felt desired and appreciated. I felt all the things I should have felt with my husband that he only gave me when we were dating.

In May 2004, I left my husband for good. I moved in with my sister. She came over to help me move and the only thing my soon-to-be-ex-husband said was, "When are you going to be done, I want to go hang out with my brother and cousin and you need to watch the kids." My sister told him to just go; she and I took the kids and moved me to her apartment.

I quickly began a secret love affair with Adam. No one had any idea. The visits to my family's house in Murrieta became more and more frequent. Secret flirting in front of everyone. It was so thrilling. Texting each other dirty thoughts and desires while we were all in the same room. It was about to grow to another level.

When the kids stayed with their dad, I would lie to my sister and tell her I was going to a girlfriend's house when, in actuality, I was driving to Murrieta in the middle of the night to pick Adam up at his house. We would wait till his parents went to bed and he would sneak out and meet me at my car and we would go to this secluded road and have sex in my car all night.

Sometimes I would still visit my family and we would all hang out and we would just pretend we were friends. My life was a gigantic lie, and I was lying to everyone in it. I was happier this way, living a free life so to say, but deep down inside the reality that if anyone ever found out tormented me; I would be in so much trouble over it. He fed my insecurities and gave me all the things I was missing with my husband; he was very good that way. I fell so deeply in love with him, more than I ever was with my ex-husband.

In true narcissistic style, he cheated on me (the first time) with his ex-girlfriend, and it devastated me. I did anything and everything in my power to get him back, groveled, begged, and told him I forgave him even though he showed little to no remorse. We continued our secret love affair. I started playing the submissive role again that I was always taught to do.

He eventually moved out of his parents' house and started spending a lot of time with some new friends and we grew distant.

We broke up, and I moved on to one of another cousin's best friends and roommate. I had grown up with him as his family and mine had been friends for many years. We quickly started a love affair as well. It was a whirlwind romance for sure. He was very animated and funny and thought I was incredibly attractive and before you know it; I was in his bed having sex.

Again, we pretended to be just friends, and nothing was happening. Every moment I spent time with him I could pretend that I wasn't suffocated by the Organization, and I could just be MYSELF. I had the attention and admiration of someone who liked me for it. Within a month or two, Adam came back around. He figured out I had "moved on" and was jealous (Another narcissistic quality. *Why wasn't I seeing the pattern yet?*)

Things ended with my cousin's roommate, and I went back to Adam. Man, was I on cloud nine knowing he loved me so much he fought to have me back. Before long he became distant again and not too long after that he told me he was going to the elders to confess all his sins and he would no longer speak to me.

We ended all communication. I was heartbroken. I loved him so deeply. Whether it was real and healthy, I still felt the emotions with all my heart. Shortly after that my father called and told me he found out what I was doing. Apparently, Adam, in his confession of his sins to the elders, admitted he was sleeping with another woman . . . also with the same name as mine at the same time as he was with me.

I couldn't breathe. I had no way of contacting him; I was devastated all over again. All my secrets came out and everyone in my family was extremely disappointed in me. They deemed me the harlot who overtook him and forced him to act and do those things because in *his* double life, he was the golden child of the congregation and the son of an elder. I was the "bad seed" living up to my name. (Mind you, this same female cousin I had been hanging out with to meet him, then dated our cousin's roommate that I had been dating and they eventually got engaged and married. I was the only one not invited to the wedding. Make it make sense, she did exactly what I just did.)

Since our divorce wasn't legal yet, I had to confess everything to my ex-husband so we could move forward and proceed with a legal and spiritual divorce.

Within the Jehovah's Witness organization, you are not allowed to divorce unless the case of adultery or death. If your mate dies, it ends the bonds of a spiritual marriage; if you and your mate decide to divorce, you can BUT you are not allowed to date or entertain any other partner until the other either dies or "commits adultery" first.

As I got older and closer to legal drinking age, I hadn't increased my intake of alcohol by that much. Granted, I drank since age thirteen but not to an extreme and at this point only with family, so it didn't register as a "problem". Also, I had a baby at nineteen and twenty-one so there was some time there when it wasn't an issue.

If I drank, I REALLY drank. Binge drinking, they call it. Once the kids' father and I got divorced and I was dealing with the breakup from Adam, it escalated. I lived my life as if I had zero responsibilities when the kids were at his house in his custody. Every other weekend I explored my individuality and learned who I was, both in and out of the Organization.

Every family gathering we had, most of which were in Orange County at my aunt and uncle's house, everyone was drinking. It was NORMAL. We made trips to the store to buy the alcohol we wanted and planned it all out beforehand to spend the night at our family's house. I passed out on toilets, on floors, blacked out in many places, and all of it was comical in our family. One time I had passed out in a bathroom at my aunt and uncle's house. My aunt took pictures, and it circulated around the family; everyone LAUGHED.

From there, I started a long list of habits. I'd have relationship after relationship, no more than six months at a time and no more than one month in-between two different people; a lot of them were out of state. It was a trend at the time to connect with other Jehovah's Witnesses across the country via MySpace. For me, I thought it was easier to continue to live a double life with us being so geographically separated; they thought so too.

I still lived a lie, pretending to be a Jehovah's Witness to keep my friends. But I would go to Witness parties and somehow always be able to find the other "bad seeds"–men who would have sex with me and have a "real relationship" with me as I saw it.

I gained the reputation as the virginity stealer and never stopped to think that was why men were interested and wanted to be physical with me. In my mind, I accepted it as I was the prettiest and most interesting in the room and what men wanted; all they wanted to be happy was sex, and I provided that.

I was so frustrated with the expectations of being a Jehovah's Witness, but I didn't want to lose everyone in my life, so I lived this double life for years. Attending meetings at the Kingdom Hall and going to all the conventions pretending I was a good witness while sleeping with any man I could get my hands on thinking it would become the relationship I needed and wanted.

During these years, I could never truly get over Adam. It was 1000x times harder than getting over and emotionally detaching from my ex-husband. When I found out he moved to Colorado, I admit I spent a whole day trying to find him and maybe contact him or just show up . . . maybe I spent two days.

Things escalated to the point I made very dangerous decisions for myself and with myself. I started cutting. I drank to the point of not being able to function. I put myself in a position where I woke up in the middle of the night to a man raping me in my sleep. I tried dating outside of the religion, but I could never share it with anyone because they were "worldly" so, the only supportive people around me were these men's friends or the friends' girlfriends.

I also experimented more with women; I got drunk and made out with women when I was out as "a joke". (Two women making out and everyone would cheer and take pictures, we've all been there.) To me, it relieved me of guilt in a weird way because it wasn't serious. But also, it reaffirmed I truly was sexually attracted to and interested in women, though it was never anything I could explore or admit in the Org.

I realized (although incorrectly) these bad things I experienced and went through resulted from me straying further and further from Jehovah's Organization. I had ventured out into the world and Satan was ruining my life and, God wasn't blessing or protecting me. These were the epitome of all the stories they told of those who left Jehovah from the district convention and circuit assembly's stage; this was my betrayal of God and the fact that I could not believe in him or obey him as I should. Every bad thing was consequence handed to me, if I came back and fell in line, everything in my life would be fixed.

To this point of my story, writing and meditating on how many times I wrote about feeling I had failed God or was defective for not believing in the Organization as I should was absolutely terrifying. It was scary realizing how much I accepted and indoctrinated in my mind and heart as shame and guilt and being a failure. *What GOD wanted his followers to feel deeply rooted negative emotions causing great consequence mentally and emotionally and causing them to hurt themselves or even want to die? How is this God?*

These thoughts sadly never entered my mind then. The only thing that did was that I was a horrible failure who needed to fix her life so "bad things" would stop happening and I would gain back Jehovah's favor and make it to paradise after Armageddon to see my grandmother again.

I started hanging out with young single Witness women my age and falling in line with what was acceptable and what was not for me. I had an innate ability to find all the people my age who were also drowning their emotional issues in entire liquor bottles every weekend.

I eventually met a man named Charles; everyone called him "Chuck". I was twenty-five, and he was twenty. We met at a New Year's Eve Party in 2008. One drink too many, we locked eyes, and that was it. We fell head over heels for each other. We saw each other every day from the day we met. I was so enamored and in love with him. I felt things for him I never felt for Adam or since Adam; we fit each other perfectly. He made me want to be a better Jehovah's Witness, and I felt like I finally understood what I needed to do and was OK with it. I wanted to be with him, and he wasn't judging me on my past as a Scarlet Lettered unbaptized harlot.

Our relationship was not well-received.

My family loved him; his family and friends all were against us. I was older. I had two kids, and he was still living at home and much younger than me. We faced controversy at every turn. The elders in his congregation started paying more attention to him and to us—trying to talk him out of it, make him realize it was all a bad idea. I don't think the elders realized that when they tried to do this to an individual who thinks they are in love—especially a male who's engaging in every sexual activity short of having actual penetrating sex—the individual will not hear the advice and it's going to push them further into the relationship.

Six months into our relationship, we decided to get married so that everyone would "leave us alone". I agreed because I loved him, and I saw myself with him, so I was just like, "OK yeah that's fine let's do that."

To live our lives as a couple, and everyone to leave us alone, was what I wanted. I was on board with being the good JW wife and just wanted to get on with it. I also was bombarded with constantly hearing how I was such a horrible choice for him to make. It further fueled my insecurities I had lived with all my life of never being a good enough person for God and His Church. No matter what I did or how good a person I was, just being good to others, it didn't matter.

Two months after that, we married. It all seemed great in the beginning and for at least six months. His family and friends started coming around because at this point, it was done. By marrying me, it took away the bad part of him dating me because we were now married, and married people have "unbelieving mates" all the time.

Now the focus was on how to get me baptized as soon as possible. They placed extra attention on me to conform and rise to the occasion of what would make this situation completely OK. It became difficult quickly, my new husband tried to take the lead as "head of the household" (which is what was required of a JW husband and my requirement was to let him) and put us almost $10k in debt. He didn't know how to manage a household; he didn't know how to manage and budget for a family with children.

Through my second marriage, the drinking continued to increase. Because although I loved my husband, I did, I knew a big part of this union happened so everyone would leave us alone.

I was now twenty-six and had two kids and he was twenty-one and fresh out of living at home. Everyone was against us being together. I was a bad influence. He was a good Christian boy. Drinking wine helped forget these things, helped me forget I was going through the motions of this marriage and continuing to be a part of this religion. In my opinion it wasn't a lot; to other people it was. I thought, *I'm over twenty-one, this is legal, I am holding a job and a home for my kids, so whatever, that's your opinion.*

During all of this, we dealt with custody arrangements with the kids' father in court. My children came home to me and thanked me for giving them a bath, and their clothes were always too small. They were sick all the time. As their mother, this mortified me; I wanted my children to be OK. It was never about taking my children from their father it was about making sure they were physically and mentally healthy.

I tried to get full custody and was denied. It devastated me. It sent me in a downward spiral, and I began drinking every night. Eventually we had to move into a small one-bedroom apartment to make ends meet and catch up on our debt. We slept on the couch every night. We had no intimacy; everything was so stressful.

I think I had been in a state of depression ever since I understood I was in something I didn't believe in. The effects of trying to maintain a life within those walls, knowing it wasn't what I truly wanted, had outward effects that didn't display until I was married for the second time.

In the back of my mind was the nagging inner voice saying to me, *"This IS IT? THIS is the rest of your life? You don't even want this!"* These things partnered with our failing home life, I became angry and withdrawn and in a state that I didn't realize was depression. Depression, to me, looked like the stereotype of lying in bed crying and being sad all the time. I knew I was unhappy; I was trying my best to convince myself that I wasn't, and that this life was what it was, and I had no other choice. It eventually took a toll on my marriage. We slowly grew apart; I think both of us were going through the motions to keep up appearances.

Then he left me.

In November 2009, my husband left me and never turned back. I had become so detached from our marriage. We had slowly come apart, and I was a miserable person to be around and be married to.

The drinking escalated, (How many more times could this escalate?) but again, still normal. I would come to my parents' house to visit, and my dad would have my favorite alcohol or beer waiting for me. Or he would say, "We are going out to dinner. I'll drive so you can drink". I can't blame anyone but myself for the ways things escalated but my environment was extremely enabling to this behavior and the normalcy of it. *So, what was the problem?*

I attempted to reach out to my husband to get a reason, anything; I never received one. I tried to reach out to the elders in our congregation for help to get him to talk to me and their response was to support whatever he wanted to say to me because he was baptized, and I wasn't. The demise of our marriage was to protect his spirituality.

To this day, he never explained the real reason he left.

I spiraled into extreme depression, anxiety, and bouts of vertigo. While I was sleeping, I pulled my hair out of my head. I was severely underweight, and I cried uncontrollably. All I knew was mental health was frowned upon in the Org. I drank nonstop to the point of blacking out and vomiting. This was the first time I contemplated suicide as an option to fix all the madness in my mind.

Being raised a Jehovah's Witness, searching outside help when it comes to mental health is extremely frowned upon. You are directed by others and the elders in the congregation to spend more time reading and meditating on the Bible to draw closer to Jehovah and He will fix all your problems. I always thought, simply being a Jehovah's Witness and being dedicated to Him made everything OK. So that meant you could take any two people devoted to God and force them to marry, and it would work out perfectly. *Why has no one ever brought that up?* Valid point it seems.

I threw myself into the religion thinking this is what would fix it. I remember one night at my lowest, three weeks after he left, I confided in the elders in my congregation and told them how much I was suffering.

The response I received was, "If you're still suffering from this then there is something you are not doing right with God and you need to figure that out and fix it." I never once returned to that Kingdom Hall nor attended regular meetings.

Even though I fought extreme lack of self-esteem, a fight I battled since I was a young teenager trying to fit into this cult and be accepted, I knew in my deepest of hearts that this was not OK. Sadly, I didn't leave out of strength but left out of defeat. I continued to let my lack of acceptance and ability to perform in the cult haunt me for the next ten years.

The very first time I remember feeling the outward effects of mental health illness was when my Uncle Shawn passed. Right before my second marriage, his health declined dramatically and quickly, and we lost him.

I always felt like he was the only one in the family with a head level enough to see every side of a situation, story, thought, and emotion. With him in the family, since my grandmother had passed, I never truly felt like a stranger or the odd one out. When he passed, it blew up my entire world.

I remember the moment it happened; it brought me back to saying goodbye to my grandmother. I was standing in the hospital. I remember the look on my aunt's face; I remember the feeling of breath completely leaving *my* body.

In the days that followed, I lost strength in my right arm. I couldn't hold anything heavier than a piece of paper. It was the weirdest sensation. There was no pain, just it being weak and powerless. The doctor told me, "I believe this is the effect of stress and anxiety." *HOW THE FUCK?!*

Anxiety? The stereotype that I knew, anxiety was someone behaving like they were going 1000 miles per hour and couldn't sit down or relax and talked a million miles per minute. That wasn't me, I was sad and devastated and clearly injured myself.

I remember the doctor gave me Ativan; man, that stuff was good. I took one of those pills and I was in an ooey-gooey dream-like state of relaxation. Soon on bad days, I was taking one of those along with a bottle or more of wine. Everything culminated from dating my second husband, everyone up in arms about our relationship, and a seemingly endless custody battle with the kids' dad. *Having a bad day?* Pop a pill and drink some wine. Problem solved.

Living with and dealing with depression and anxiety stemming from my divorce (and really from all of my fucking life) fed into the idea that I was not good enough which I struggled with ever since I was young. I felt as if I was forgotten as the youngest child. My body was defective, having to wear the full body brace to correct it. I didn't believe in the indoctrination that was being shoved down my throat since birth, and now even trying to be the person I was "supposed to be" didn't work. And my husband left me because I was so messed up as a person: worthless and defective.

As an adult visiting my parents' home one weekend, I walked down the hallway in their home. The wall of pictures; most likely everyone has one in their family home as well. Mom had been adding to this wall for probably over ten years. High school portraits of my mom and my dad, graduation pics of my sister, and even entire framed collages of each of my kids. I have seen this wall for over ten years, the same wall.

This particular day I realized, after all these years, there was not one single photo of me on this wall. I stood there and stared for a few minutes searching everywhere trying to find myself . . . I was not there. In that moment, it struck me so hard; I was speechless.

I couldn't say I was hurt; I think I was numb. Numb and not surprised. My default was to result to sarcasm when it comes to pain, so I remember immediately going to my mom and turning this revelation into a joke. She told me there was no way it was true. She walked into the hallway, and made the same revelation for herself. Sure enough, that next weekend I walked down that hallway and there was an entire collage dedicated to me. I couldn't decide whether that was more or less insulting than the discovery that I was missing in the first place.

Drinking became a way to escape. I lived with this nagging feeling that I was a failure and defective because I didn't believe in the religion, and drinking was a way to forget about that. Still, I never had it at home, I would only do it if I went out or was at my aunt's or parents' house, and it was sporadic. I never got behind the wheel of a car. I was always safe.

As time passed, I got older and more aware of my life slipping by, wasting it on the unhappiness of being unable to be myself. I drank more and more; I still held a job and an apartment, never was arrested, never got behind the wheel.

I mostly self-medicated with wine. Every night. I used it to relax. *What was the problem with that?* I drank and I got really goofy and funny and enjoyed myself. In those moments, I could forget all the thoughts haunting my mind and ways that I would never be good enough.

I didn't believe in the way I was raised. I had two failed marriages by twenty-seven; I had no career. I felt like a LOSER, constantly shoving myself into these misshapen round holes that people made for me when I was a square all along.

Trying to have a romantic relationship was a disaster. I become so intensely and immediately attached to the other human being but when there was the slightest change in their behavior, I freaked out, became paranoid and begged them not to leave me. Shortly after these behaviors started, the relationships ended.

It was a cycle. I would be a hateful, mean person saying the ugliest things you could ever say to someone, and the next day begging for them to come back. This went on over and over and over until the guy finally made it impossible for me to communicate with them anymore.

After many years, I realized, I was so unhappy living my life as a lie to everyone. I needed to take a step back and actually make MYSELF happy without worrying of the consequences or what anyone else might think. But it was never that easy, and I could never make that happen. The guilt and shame of that idea prevented me from ever following through, I would always revert to falling back in line of what they expected of me, reminding myself I needed to be able to see my grandmother again.

During the time I was married to my second husband, I worked with a man who was gay named Michael. At this point in time, my experience with people who are gay was limited because of the indoctrination they fed me that it was an entirely shameful and dirty way of life. Michael was my first TRUE friend I believe.

He was by my side when my husband left and when the elders treated me like I was a defective, evil non-baptized piece of shit; he picked me up off the floor and carried me along. He listened to my deepest woes, and I listened to his.

Sharing with me how his life has been, he too was involved with a strict religion. When he came out, the church shunned him and kicked him out. He shared with me what it was like to live as someone who identified as gay, and the things he endured doing so; being treated as second class, dirty, defective, and every negative description you can think of. Rejected by his family for living his true self; I not only felt such a familiar connection with him but with those in the LGBT community (as it was referred to during this time).

Michael treated me like a human being with feelings who would never be judged. He showed me what unconditional love felt like and what it meant to be a genuine friend. To this day, I don't think I would have ever made it through some points in my life if I had not met him.

During this time of self-exploration and dipping my toes fully into the pool of being a "worldly person", I started a relationship with a childhood friend. His sister and I were very close as teenagers and I babysat their younger brother. I always knew he had a crush on me when we were kids, but he was four years younger, and I never saw him that way. We all lost touch with each other for several years and reconnected in our twenties. He became one of my very good friends.

After my second husband left, he and I became closer and closer, and things grew past friendship, but we were both so terrified to make a move on it. It was comforting and calming to be interested in someone who was out of the organization yet still could relate to what it was like being raised in it.

I vividly remember the first time he came to my apartment after our friendship turned into more than just a friendship; I remember exactly where we were the first time he kissed me.

Our relationship was amazing, we knew each other so well, and we had known each other for so many years it was so easy to be with him. His mother told us, she had always wanted me to be with him and always knew I was the one for him. We made plans to get married in Rome one day.

Being divorced without scriptural ground, I was not allowed to date so we kept our relationship secret from anyone who might tell the elders and get us in trouble. Even though we were not active in the congregations, it was still the risk of being found out and our families and others shun us out of their lives. It was beautiful until it wasn't, for most of the relationship we carried on as if we weren't in this cult and we were free to be ourselves and have a normal relationship.

Eventually, it became noticeable. I still remember the day my brother confronted me. We were in his car, and he brought up how it was wrong that we were dating; how it was wrong in God's eyes and how bad we looked to him, that it was all inappropriate. When we got back to my parents' house where I was visiting, I flew into a full-blown panic attack, gathering all my things as fast as I could while screaming and crying, hot tears streaming down my face.

How can a God I am supposed to love, and who loves me not support my happiness and see how happy I am? How can my family not support me? Once again, it fed into the narrative that I was a useless, defective fuckup.

He started getting cold feet about how serious we were; he didn't want to leave his mother since he lived with her and took care of her. We drifted apart, and I became very angry. I started being mean to him. I took out on him not only the frustrations I felt toward him, but everything I felt toward my second husband, since I never got to have that conversation with him and express my feelings. He took the brunt of everything.

Not only did I lose another love, but I also lost the first person I was romantically involved with that understood what it was like to be raised this way. I knew it wasn't for him and he was struggling the same ways I was with the constant push and pull in which direction to go. He, in my eyes, was the most perfect scenario of a person for me to spend my life with. FINALLY, SOMEONE GOT IT, and I still found a way to fuck it all up. So now I'm REALLY a colossal failure of a human being was how it seemed.

Coinciding with the end of this relationship, I started school to get my cosmetology license. Although I always held jobs and socialized with co-workers who weren't Jehovah's Witnesses and having this friendship with Michael, I was given the opportunity to be social with so many others who were not only *not* Jehovah's Witnesses, but on the same path I was, a path to a new beginning.

My depression and anxiety deepened from the failure of this last relationship, and I escaped by truly living a double life. Living a life of freedom, to be who I was without judgement; it was so freeing and beautiful. I had always wanted this feeling but in the back of my mind was the guilt that I was committing a grave and unforgiveable sin. Even though I no longer attended the congregation, I continued to live this double life in front of my family for years so I would not lose them, so they wouldn't shun me forever. The innate feeling of wanting to be loved and accepted by your family I don't think ever goes away. My love and desire to have it overwhelmed the confidence I had to truly be myself so, the only reasonable action WAS to live a double life.

I had always wanted to do hair my whole life and never thought I would be able to because I had two kids and had to work to support my family. I went to school part time for two years, collecting unemployment and my parents supporting me financially. The entire time I was in school I was single, I told myself if I was really going to change, I needed to change everything.

OK, I would hook up with guys here and there because this was around the time online dating started and what was a lonely emotionally and mentally messed up girl to do?

When my kids were with me, I spent time with them, not going out. I often spent this time at my parent's home helping my brother take care of the household. Both of my parents were now partially disabled, and my brother took care of them. I came every other weekend to relieve him of these duties so he could have a break; I would clean the house, grocery shop, take my mother to crafting classes. It always bothered me that my other siblings rarely, if ever, came to help or spend time with our parents. They had other grandchildren who rarely visited and if they did, it was for just a few brief hours, and they would leave.

When they were at their dad's, I would spend time with friends I made at my previous job, and girls I had made friends with at school. It was so refreshing to have this friend circle that was nonjudgmental of me. These friends from various backgrounds widely accepted me.

We went and enjoyed our time, drinking heavily and laughing about it the next day. I was finally in a good place and to be honest, I truly believed I was. Nothing could ever be perfect. My personal life was seemingly amazing but to my family, none of this stuff was even happening. I lied or avoided conversations about what I was doing and when or I lied about attending meetings. At this point, I only attended the Memorial of Jesus Christ's Death every year with my parents (a super important event and celebration much like the celebration of Easter) but I lied to them stating I was still going to meetings.

Every Sunday I would get the same text message or phone call from my mother, "How did you enjoy the talk today?" or "How did you enjoy this week's Watchtower Study?" Sometimes I would lie; sometimes I told her I didn't go. She would reply, "Well there's always next week." I did this song and dance for years with her out of the fear that she would abandon me; I was too scared to tell her I was living a completely worldly lifestyle now.

When my oldest brother left and joined the Army (an act that my entire family still rallied around him), mom started telling people she had three kids, not four. I never forgot that, and I didn't want my mom telling people she had three kids again.

Achieving completion of trade school and having secular education outside of general education was also a monumental feat as a Jehovah's Witness. I had reached a point where, instead of looking back on my divorce and life obstacles as painful, I looked at them as events that brought me to this point with gratitude instead of anger.

They awarded me a certificate, and I was going to walk a graduation at a COLLEGE. This was AMAZING. I reached out to my family in excitement to tell them of the day and time of the graduation. I purchased my cap and gown.

The only response I received was, they would not come. It was, "too far and on a bad day for them, *blah, blah, blah*", whatever the FUCK their reason was. You know who had also gone through trade school years before and graduated and the ENTIRE FAMILY attended? My oldest brother.

Because of this rejection, I never walked at my graduation. I attended the ceremony in support of my other classmates though. I remember sitting by myself and feeling like every bad thought and emotion I had ever felt about myself in my family's eyes was undoubtedly accurate. I don't think I could ever express how heart shattering this moment was for me. It may seem like nothing, but it wasn't nothing to me. It was a culmination of every awful moment of how I was treated by my family and confirmation I was nothing.

So, I turned to love to fill that hole.

Right at the end of school I met a man named Danny. We had an amazing connection immediately and related to each other very well. He was born and raised in the Mormon Church and had difficulty with his family accepting him no longer being a part of the religion; the same way I felt for many years with the Jehovah's Witness religion.

We had a fast and hard romance; I had never been so sexually connected to someone since Adam and that floored me. Anytime we were out in public strangers used to ask us how many years we had been together when in fact it had been only a few months. Not only were we connected on many levels, including both being raised in a high control religion, but we were also out of said religions.

I saw now that I trauma bonded to him or perhaps; we did to each other. I grabbed on to him to show me the way and validate what I was doing, not being a JW. Since he did it and his life was great; it was going to be OK.

It came crashing down the night of my graduation party from Cosmetology School. He was distant and weird. At the end of the night, we went back to my apartment, and he fell asleep. I knew something wasn't right, and he had spent about 90% of the night on his phone texting someone. I went through his phone. He had been texting his ex-girlfriend saying how much he wanted to be with her and wished he could be with her right now to have sex with her.

I became enraged and kicked him out of my apartment at 3am. I was so hurt but hated that someone else was "better" than me and I became obsessed with having him back and being the one he wanted (this went on for two years off and on). We had only actually dated maybe four months. I became obsessed with "what's wrong with me", why couldn't I have a good relationship even though I had made all these changes for myself and finally started living for myself instead of just living a huge lie all the time. But to be honest, I was still living the lie of a double life and was lying to myself that I was living for myself. I was horribly and unendingly inundated with the emotions of guilt and shame and failure and just never spoke about it.

After I graduated, I worked at my first salon in Pasadena, California. It was the best year of my life so far. I never felt so strong, empowered, useful, meaningful, fulfilled. Everything was so good; I made amazing friends and had an amazing career. I had formed friendships; I was entirely honest about my life and upbringing and the battles I dealt with my family of trying to be accepted by them. They loved me regardless and not only was I loved, but they supported, encouraged, and told me how amazing and wonderful I was.

This was something I had never experienced in my life. I had never had people in my life treat me and express to me that exactly *WHO I WAS*, was an amazing, accepted person. I had so many amazing opportunities come my way professionally because of this job and these people. My career was the main focus of my life, other than my children.

In my first salon, I was lucky enough to be chosen as the salon Muse and started modeling and having my picture put in a local popular edgy Los Angeles magazine as the ad for the salon. I got extra copies of every magazine, and ANYTHING published I was in for my mom. She was my biggest fan and was so proud of what I was doing with my career. I had finally received some sort of acceptance and pride from her. I was finally doing something right.

During Fashion Week, I went to Bellevue, Washington to model in a show for *Vogue Magazine*. I called my mom from my hotel room as I stared out the window before I was due for hair and makeup, told her I loved her and wished she was there to see it. A part of me felt like I had "made it". I was doing something of worth. I finally gained love from a parent who was proud of what I was doing.

No one in my life up to this moment showed me acceptance. I had lived every day feeling like what I did was never enough, that I was a flawed person and could never put myself 100% into the good graces of being accepted by her or anyone.

I felt on the top of the world. I was successful with this career even though I was told my whole life that I was to keep a minimal job and not be successful, that my time was better served in the ministry and all glory belonged only to Jehovah. It showed me that, being away from the Organization wasn't what caused bad things to happen. It made it easier for me to accept that lie. A romantic relationship wasn't important to me during this period; it was more about enjoying my life. I was growing as a person in leaps and bounds.

Expressing myself through my looks and clothing, really pushing the envelope and enjoying the freedom became my new way of life. My hair eventually made its way into being a multicolored mohawk and I was HERE FOR IT. I will never forget the day I was given the name, "Pony".

"You look just like a My Little Pony! I'm going to start calling you Pony," I could still hear the owner of the salon say (she became one of my very dear friends). This name was adopted without my choice or approval, not that I minded entirely. It became the moment I could attach a name to this new person I was becoming. My family knew me and called me my birth name and everyone else in this new life I was trying to figure out and build referred to me as "Pony".

Pony was amazing. Pony was strong and resilient and confident and lovable and fun and every single positive descriptive compliment I could think of. Pony was ME as a free person. My birth name no longer served me any purpose and had become detestable. My new life was beautiful.

I could never go long without having some sort of "attention" from a male that I was interested in. It couldn't be any male, it had to be someone I was interested in as well and if it didn't happen hard and fast, then it was never strong enough to hold my attention for longer than a day. I would frequent dating sites and apps just looking for that next high of attention and entertain it for a day or two, get bored, and repeat. At times I'd leave the sites and apps alone for a couple days, weeks or months, and repeat.

Seven months into this new life of freedom I met Robert.

Robert and I met on Plenty of Fish; he lived 250 miles away in Mammoth Lakes, California. Our connection was strong, fierce, passionate, wild and everything you could ever want from someone. It was sudden and intense. We talked all the time, every day. About four weeks into talking, texting, and face timing, he came down to visit me in person.

He was everything I dreamed he would be. We fit together perfectly, and I thought I had finally found the person I was going to spend my life with. He was a single father with majority custody of his two sons, a hard worker, and very close with his family, all ideal qualities any woman would love. He visited me twice; I visited him once.

Our relationship was rocky periodically; I had little confidence that he was actually being faithful to me, which fueled me to want him even more. We got into several arguments over his associations with other woman, other "friends". My friends were leery of him mostly because they would see me cry over him.

Over the first three months of getting to know each other, Robert mentioned he was moving back to Las Vegas. He had lived there for a few years working with the union as a cement mason. He left because the work had dramatically slowed, and he could have better employment with his father back in Mammoth. Apparently work would soon pick up again and he would have great employment through the Union. He told me to move to Las Vegas with him; he sold me on the way of living there (cost of living was lower compared to LA), we would be together, and it would help us provide a better life for ourselves and our children.

That was the most enticing part to me because I was living in a one-bedroom apartment in the Pasadena area I could barely afford. I would sleep on the couch every night because I didn't have a bedroom or even a bed of my own. My one bedroom was completely dedicated and outfitted for the kids. This new life was what I wanted. I would move to Las Vegas with the man I loved and be able to see the kids more with the new custody arrangement I proposed. I could save money to better support the kids as they got older. I was confident that in time they would want to be with me full-time anyway.

I quickly decided this was what I wanted to do and informed my parents and family. I remember telling my dad and he kind of held his head down for a minute and then looked at me and said, "I think this is a great idea for you to have a better life and be able to support yourself." I was SHOCKED. My dad went even as far as to pay for my gas and hotel room to visit Las Vegas before moving to go on interviews so I could have a job when I arrived.

At this time as well, I petitioned the court to revisit and alter our custody agreement to accommodate this move. It was a much lengthier process than I had imagined. Things got difficult between Robert and me. He became distant and treated me as more of an annoyance than a help and support. He was having trouble finding work in Las Vegas even though he claimed the Union told him to come back because they had so much work for them. It took me so long to move that he accused me of not being there for him.

I begged and pleaded with him not to be upset with me or distant with me. My text messages and phone calls were ignored. Finally, the relationship ended, and he broke up with me. This happened the day before I was supposed to move all my stuff into storage and after I gave my property management word that I was moving out. They had already found a new tenant for my apartment. I also was giving up the amazing career I had built here for myself doing hair.

This, along with the fact that I secured a place to live in Las Vegas already, made me determined to follow through with my plan. To be honest, I had grown tired of California, and now dedicated to the idea of providing a better life for my kids this way. I moved all my stuff into storage and lived the last week in my apartment sleeping on the floor with whatever would fit in my car to go with me.

That week Robert reached out to me. He was upset things hadn't worked out for him and was going to move back to Mammoth. I asked him to come back to me. I told him I had a house, and we could live together. He agreed. I moved to Vegas with what I could pack into my four-door Chevy Tracker, leaving all my belongings behind in storage.

When I left, the adjusted custody arrangement was still pending, and I was still seeing the kids for an entire week every month. I went to the library every day applying for jobs (I had no Wi-Fi at the house) and tried to get adjusted to my new life in Las Vegas. Shortly after moving the relationship with my parents and family became extremely strained, and they were no longer supportive of this decision OR me.

I also learned quickly that the reason Robert and I really broke up when he first moved to Vegas was because he was seeing an old girlfriend. He caught himself in his own lies many times repeating stories; when he first told it he was alone, and in the new version of these stories he referred to "we".

So here I am, alone, in Las Vegas, zero friends, and I learn that my boyfriend who just moved in, that I have known for four months, was cheating on me. *So what did I do?* I stayed . . . and became obsessed with being like this other woman who caused him to want her instead of me. Then, the final hearing for my children's custody confirmed, and life has never been the same since.

June 13, 2014

I walked into court expecting everything to go my way. The new custody plan would be approved, and I would move on with my life, our lives–the kids and me. We waited our turn in family court and when the time finally came, the judge asked for the entire courtroom to be emptied. Only my ex-husband and I were to be present in the courtroom other than all the people involved on the court's side.

This had never happened before, I was concerned and confused. The judge called the social worker involved with our case to give testimony over speakerphone. I was still confused. She testified that my father, brother and sister, children's father, and many members of his family told her I was an "unfit mother" for my children; I had always made bad decisions in my life, I hung out with bad influences, I strayed into another direction in my life, and I had a drinking problem.

Over the few weeks since I moved to Las Vegas, it became apparent I was completely out of the Jehovah's Witness organization and at this point it was a full-blown effort to take the children from me to save them from their worldly mother.

It blindsided me. I was terrified and so confused. I heard the social worker testify my son had told her I had a drinking problem, that he once saw a friend and me drink an entire twenty-four pack of beer in one night and that I was drunk (I still stand by the fact this never happened and I know the exact event he was speaking of, but regardless).

I was pissed. I was so angry. My entire WORLD AND LIFE had turned their back on me, and I had a drinking problem? Every time I went to my parents' house my father had already bought me liquor or immediately gave me money and told me to go get some or if we went out to dinner, it was "I'll drive so you can have some drinks," not even a question.

There were statements which encouraged and supported all angles of my "drinking". I was well over twenty-one, never had a DUI, always taken care of my responsibilities, and now it was being thrown in my face? And my sister? We hadn't had a relationship in almost two years. She was no longer a part of my life.

I tried to defend myself and the judge looked at me and said, "If everyone in your life is saying these things about you, they must be true." He would not listen to anything I had to say. I sat there crying, the bailiff brought me tissues.

Then I learned my fate. I could no longer see my children. They gave me the right to have dinner with them that night and after that no contact. The judge told me to consider seeking treatment and if I wanted to contest the ruling, I could return with character witnesses on my behalf.

I looked at him and said, "You want me to bring the same people to testify on my behalf that are the reasons you're taking my kids from me now?" Since one reason was the associations I was keeping, how could I bring them on my behalf? That comment wasn't well received.

I walked out of that courtroom in a daze. I felt like life wasn't real; I wasn't real. This was a dream. This was a mistake. My level of confusion was indescribable. I stood in the hallway with Robert, crying, and telling him everything. Both of us were so angry and hurt. My life was over. It was so over.

Replaying the last couple of interactions with my family in my mind, there was a time my father was watching the kids for me and took them to my sister's house and left them there without asking or telling me.

When I protested, he told me, "If you don't leave them there, I will fucking kill you."

Then one day my son came home from school with a horrible attitude and when I sat him down and asked what was wrong, why he was so upset, he looked at me and said, "YOU'RE DISGUSTING!" He explained that his father and stepmother told *my* children that because I didn't love Jehovah, I was a disgusting person and evil.

Why didn't I see this coming, but better yet WHY WAS THIS HAPPENING? IN WHAT WORLD WAS THIS LEGAL OR OK OR ALLOWED?

After court, I had dinner with the kids that night at our favorite restaurant where we would go as a little family. I tried to keep the conversation as normal as possible, although their dad and stepmom had already told them their version of what happened.

All the while, I could only think, this was my last meal with my children. This was the last time hearing their laughs, seeing them smile, smelling what they smell like, feeling their touch and embracing them. The torment inside me was unmeasurable and indescribable. I was utterly, completely broken beyond repair.

I took one last picture of them.

I have it to this day.

I got in my car and watched them walk away from me until I could see them no more. I replay that moment in my head, and it haunts me to this day, over and over. Remembering the last time I saw their faces. My life.

June 14, 2014

We drove back to Vegas and all I thought was, *I literally just lost everyone in my life: my kids and my entire family have now shunned me. All of them were gone.* I was numb. I was in this weird daze as if I was high on 1000 pills. It wasn't real, it certainly didn't feel real.

Everything reminded me of everyone. Imagine having to mourn fifteen people at once as if they were dead, when you know well enough, they were still alive. Imagine living with the realization that, everything you had ever known was ripped from you and was gone, that your family discarded you, your parents–the ones who were to love you always, no matter what.

I was living my life as a worldly person choosing this lifestyle over the life of being a Jehovah's Witness and a drunk who made bad decisions and therefore was a harm to my children. I was so broken inside, in so much pain. I had lost my children, my family–my only known support system and social environment.

I numbed everything with alcohol. I didn't care. All the time, I cried. All I did was drink. If I wasn't working, I was drinking. On the weekends, all day long. I clung tighter to this relationship that had grown abusive. I did not have enough love or respect for myself to change this narrative, as if I deserved it and the drinking made life bearable.

It affected me deeply; it affected my relationship deeply. We fought constantly; I pushed him away. He took advantage of my brokenness; we broke up and got back together ten times. He moved out, moved back in. Cheated on me multiple times.

At first when I found out I was mad and then that quickly turned into, "I don't care." I didn't want him to leave me, so I begged for him to come back, going along with anything he wanted. I was in this horrible relationship with this completely narcissistic man whom I couldn't leave because then I would REALLY be alone. Holding on to this disgustingly painful and abusive relationship because I deserved nothing good in life; I deserved to suffer and be miserable. Getting drunk every night allowed me to be sexual with him. I had zero inhibitions.

He had so many issues with me. I was not very good at connecting with his youngest child; I had no desire to. I didn't even have my own kids. The kid disliked me, Robert saw that. We fought over money. We fought over being physical with each other.

One night he threatened to burn down the house with me in it. I ran outside and called the police. He ran and hid from them. We threw things at each other. I had never been in a relationship in my life that was "physical"; I had never acted "physical" with anyone before.

I got drunk and assaulted him outside of a casino because he did nothing for my birthday; I left him at the casino and drove home in his car, drunk. He showed up the next morning after having walked fifteen miles all night and had a black eye. He pushed me and I fell into a wall, but I stayed with this man, regardless.

I had no self-respect. He would put my images on websites advertising wanting to bring another female into our bedroom. I got mad when I found out and then got drunk and conceded.

He put us on Craigslist advertising that we were looking for a third person to be sexual with together. Sending explicit pictures of me to these other women, he texted them from his phone in secret, planning for them to come over. I would come home to women in our home waiting for me to come home to have sex with them while he watched. I so badly wanted someone to LOVE ME and ACCEPT ME.

All the while I was a horrible person to be around. I was a miserable person, created problems left and right and then begged for forgiveness. He cheated on me many times. Through all this, I couldn't let him go. I think mainly because I loved him, but I knew no one else in Las Vegas, and he was there with me when everything happened. I attached to him all of those moments and if I lost him, then I lost everything all over again. I'd lose the attachment to my children because he was there in court with me, and I couldn't stand to lose anyone else in my life.

I threw myself into moving on with my life and tried getting stable employment.

I applied to work at a Chiropractic office since most of my work experience before going to Cosmetology School was based in office work. I got a call back to interview, and that's when I met Desarae.

Desarae tells the story that she immediately liked me because I reminded her of the singer Pink and she thought I was cool. (A story we still laugh about to this day). We bonded quickly in a kindred spirit way. As we learned more about each other, we found out we had many life events and stories that were similar in so many ways.

Her story related to mine so well but different enough that we weren't identical. We weren't trauma bonding; I developed a close friendship with her and could pour my heart out. Desarae would hold space for me as one should in a family, as a best friend, as someone who loves me unconditionally. My journey began as she taught and showed me what that type of love really meant and what it looked like.

During this time, my boyfriend and I started therapy, couples therapy. He still attested to the fact that he was absolutely in love with me and wanted to save this relationship. Little did I know at the time that this would be the best thing that ever happened to me.

He chose the therapist; her name was Jillian. Her office was in walking distance of our house. I quickly bonded with her and felt completely comfortable and at ease speaking with her. Though even initially the idea of it was daunting since in the back of my mind I was raised to believe that any mental health care or help was WRONG.

It quickly became apparent to both Jillian and Desarae; I was in a dangerous relationship with a narcissistic man. Jillian called me on a random Saturday afternoon to tell me she discussed my case with her supervisor, and they were both worried about my safety; I needed to get away from him. After sharing this information with Desarae, she told me it was time; she had my back and would help me with anything I needed. Her family was now my family; I would never be alone. With the help of Desarae and Jillian, I could leave him for good.

It took me a long time to get away from him completely. Even when I did, every six months to a year, I would unblock his number, he would contact me, come over, and we would get drunk and have sex all night. Once we woke up the next morning, we would fight, and he'd go home to his girlfriend. We wouldn't see each other again for another six months to a year. This was something I fought fiercely never to admit or let Desarae ever know. I feared she would eject me out of her family just as my blood relatives had shown was so easy to do; she would surely do it just as easily if not easier.

I threw myself into therapy. It still felt super foreign to me, and I felt a little guilty. But also, I felt I was in a moment of attaching myself to something that could fix me. Going to therapy also made me feel like I could open up and someone would softly explain to me I wasn't a waste of a human being. The words she chose resonated with me and landed softly even if they were things I didn't want to hear. She explained and showed me the things I had been through were actual traumas and the results they had on me were essentially, OK. I wasn't broken or defective from what happened to me.

I learned so much about mental health and diagnoses; I started exploring that world on my own as well. Looking back on it, I don't know if that was what I needed to do. I don't recommend going out and googling "mental health" and trying to diagnose yourself, it will probably bring back results that you have cancer and are dying.

One day we had a session, I looked at her and said, "Is there a book I can read about this?" All throughout my childhood I was a lover of books and always would be reading something. I enjoyed learning through written word, and I felt it was the best way for me to process and retain information. She never had anyone ask her that before and she said, "I will find it and tell you."

That quickly became my go to. I threw myself into self-help books. One book led to another, led to another. Then led by my intuition, into books on spirituality, healing crystals, Myers-Briggs, Enneagram, DiSC, anything by Caroline Myss, *The Four Agreements, The Celestine Prophecy,* Narcissistic Lovers, (by the way all of these are fantastic theories and books). I even developed a fascination with Sigmund Freud.

I grew in knowledge and became rich in friendships. Four of the friends I made working in the Pasadena salon were still by my side and were now my family; in Vegas I made more family. When I wasn't working, I spent all my time with Desarae and her family; I was their fifth family member. The time I spent in Vegas will always be my favorite. To this day I truly feel Las Vegas is my home and not LA.

Desarae's family showed me what being a family meant, showed me what unconditional love meant, and what it looked like. They showed me I could reciprocate to them and build that love with others. I began to trust again and felt worthy.

I had fun, too much fun. I spent my nights with friends laughing and drinking and dancing. Every

Friday night we had "Parker House Party". Everyone came to the house, and we played darts in the garage, shot gunned beers, played cornhole in the street, were goofy, and made the best memories I ever had. I was in a place where I felt I had healed. I was happy about the fact that now I was finally completely myself with people without hiding and they loved me for it. Even though sometimes it was overwhelming and terrifying, I would have left this earth sooner if it weren't for them.

Everything was fun; reality was not a thing at the time.

Don't get me wrong, I did not write this lightly to convey that once I started therapy and got some good friends the clouds parted, and I was healed. What I'm saying is there was enough around to distract me from what I was battling inside, to make me believe I was fine. Although I had lost my family, I gained myself and that carried me along for some time.

I enjoyed times of freedom, learning about myself and what I liked and didn't like. The feeling of being completely free to be myself was very fulfilling. Not entirely fulfilling, but it was a large part of my life that I still look back in fondness and enjoyed regardless of the events that handed it to me. I made good friends with a man who identified as LGBT and started spending much more time in that community and with him.

To be honest, to this day it's my favorite community to be in. I have never been in a place where everyone around me accepted everyone else. We all drank, laughed, and had fun—no one was trying to hit on everyone else. We were all glad and proud to be in a place where we were WELCOME.

He showed me that I could be a thing out in the world. He was an only child and now really, so was I; we coined the nicknames Brother and Sister almost immediately. He was the brother I always wanted and the best friend in a sibling I had lost, but he was better. He had a lot of the same struggles as I and some rough times with his family accepting him for who he was. At the end of the day his family accepted and loved him.

Although for different reasons, I too was searching in my life for the same high he was living. After being raised in a cult, I didn't believe this life was possible and felt like I was never good enough. He wasn't perfect either. He struggled and had bad days, and on the days he was down I picked him up and vice versa.

I am not expanding on the "relationships" I had while in this town. I promise you; you already know who and what they entailed, which was another entirely frustrating and constantly soul crushing aspect of my life. How after all this time and books read, was I still repeating the same mistakes with the same people romantically?

No one can fix it all with a drink in one hand and a book in the other; the more I couldn't fix things the angrier I got. It became harder to leave my bed. Making the right decisions was more difficult. It was harder to love myself and easier to push those things away.

The reality was I was spinning faster and faster down the drain of ruining my life. My relationship with alcohol became so strong that it seemed more important than my best friendships. The truth was, I continued to drink and shove all the trauma down. I stopped therapy because I thought I was OK. The nights when I was going out drinking, I'd hang out with the wrong people and was careless with myself physically.

I met a man who I barely knew, a friend of a friend of a friend. He was in town from back east; he knew I had lived there, so he asked me to come meet up with his friends and him. Drinking allowed me to be carefree and have fun; I couldn't remember how to have fun without drinking. While his friends watched, I had sex with this man in a jacuzzi hot tub. I found myself in strip clubs being molested by women. One time a club manager gave me a ride home in his Ferrari because they left me in the club with no way home; I felt I owed this man something, so I gave him a blowjob in his car.

I went out and had fun with my friends but the next day the overwhelming guilt made it impossible for me to get out of bed. It made me constantly frustrated because I read all the books, bought all the crystals, believed in all the agreements, and still wasn't healed. This was bullshit. I was still and would always be defective. At this low point, I never held a job for even a year in one place.

My closest friend who carried me through most of this became distant. To this day I'm not entirely sure why, but I chalked it up to the fact that I had spread my wings and became comfortable being myself in life. I also made more friends who were single like me. She had a family of four and couldn't go out and do the things I was now doing. I felt she resented me for growing and I resented her for not being happy for me for it.

We grew apart, and my allegiance to her faded. Subconsciously I created a divide between us so she could dispose of me since I felt she was already going to. Instead of directly addressing the elephant in the room, I caused it to run away. I was never taught that I could do something wrong, and someone would still want me. I grew into this horrible version of myself that was worse than the day I arrived there. She and her family never gave me a reason to feel like I couldn't confide deeply or as if I was a defective member of this family, but my trauma did. The resounding voice in the back of my mind reminded me I was not worthy of that love.

I made a terrible choice to trust someone I barely knew and gave them a place to live in my home. They were going through a hard time, and I felt moved to help since I had a soft heart for those who were struggling; I had been in that place many times. The situation quickly became dangerous and violent, culminating as they orchestrated a full robbery of my home. At first glance, it looked like someone had kind of ransacked the place. They threw things around, but my big TV was still in the living room right by the front door, so something didn't add up.

When the cops arrived, I explored further and found all my jewelry was gone. All the jewelry from my grandmother, all my children's birth certificates, all the digital cameras and memory cards containing all their pictures, almost every single sentimental material artifact I had of my former life was stolen.

It was all gone. The last tangible pieces for me to touch and see from my former life, were gone.

Shame was all I felt. Words failed me in recounting and trying to express this moment. They replay in my mind to this day. I was in a worse place than when I arrived in that town after losing what I thought was everything. THIS was losing IT ALL.

It was exactly a week later when that roommate also had my car stolen from the parking lot of my job. *Now,* I had lost it all.

I destroyed the friendship with the woman who saved me from going into a complete wasteland after everything happened with my family. She and her family showed me what a family REALLY meant, and I shit on it all with alcohol and selfishness.

Everything became too heavy and once again my plan of action was to run. One of my core friends had moved to Nashville, Tennessee two years before and wanted me to come too. "Move here you will love it," she said. So, I left Vegas.

I moved to Nashville to escape, but the problems followed. I couldn't leave trauma in another state, it came with me. So along with trauma, I brought my extreme alcoholism.

When I moved to Tennessee, I moved in with a friend I had considered a sister and the results were disastrous, the energy and time living together was toxic and dangerous for both of us. The first thing I did after finding a job was to find a man/relationship to throw myself into.

I successfully convinced myself that all was fine in the world now; I moved to this beautiful new state I loved, away from all my problems and got an awesome new job. Life was amazing. This was all I needed to function.

I felt like this was the part of the story where there was a pause, and a deep male voice would say, "In fact all was NOT GOOD in her world."

Stuck in an endless circle of, getting drunk, finding a man, hanging out with friends, going to work, became my normal. For about two years, these were the only things I accomplished.

I made friends with a narcissistic woman with ties to the music industry and I felt like a rockstar with her. I adopted her success as my own and would tell myself, "Look at me now, if only my family and those who disowned me could see me now." This friendship made me feel I had suddenly WON at life, and everything was OK. In reality, I had once again succumbed to the grasp of another clever narcissistic person. This time, under the guise of a woman; though I would not figure it out for some time.

The only bright moment during this era was Desarae and I repaired our friendship after months apart. She was back in my life and she and her family still loved me, regardless.

One night during this time, I sent a Facebook message to my mother (heavily intoxicated and emotional) telling her I missed her. A year later, I was sitting on the couch of my apartment watching a movie with my boyfriend and got a notification on my phone that she had messaged me. "I miss you too, babygirl." I replied to it although I don't remember what I said, and she never replied.

She was so unforgiving of imperfection; the standards she held me to as her daughter and being raised in the organization, I would never suffice them no matter what I did. If I ever came to her with an issue or a problem wanting to vent, it would be met with, "Pray to Jehovah, that will fix it,". This response caused me to be so resentful of prayer because sometimes you just want your mom to empathize and help problem solve or tell you, "You are doing your best and it's ok". But all I ever got was, "Pray to Jehovah, Jehovah will fix it."

The level of how much I miss her is deadly. There have been so many moments since we have not spoken where my first instinct was to call her and tell her what I did, or what I saw, or whatever the experience was, and I couldn't. I still grasped for an invisible acceptance I would never be granted. That fact haunts me every day, that is the reality I face currently.

How could you dispose of your own child as a mother and not try, not fight for me? Then again, that's what I did with my own kids; I didn't fight enough for them. So maybe it all comes back around to me repeating the behavior that was shown me. Not an excuse by any means, nor am I a victim as I stand proudly in my story. However, somehow somewhere I had to start taking little pieces of things to compile reasons how this all happened to begin with. Creating and crafting my closure to keep myself from going crazy, except that version of closure never worked for me either. It stung and hurt as much as the truth of the situation most likely would.

People presented me with the response: "Your parents just did the best they could with what they knew," to help subside my pain, to try showing me I needed to give them grace for leaving me. My response to this was, "You mean to tell me as a parent, you didn't know better to not abandon one of your own children?"

I refused to accept this answer; it brought me no comfort and was a completely invalid excuse. Then again, here I am using that as my own excuse for why I didn't fight harder for my kids, leaving them to think they were better off without me and making that decision because it was the best decision I could make in that moment with what I knew. I have always been torn why I felt like I was justified being in that "place," but it couldn't be justified for MY parents. This was a never-ending merry-go-round of right-wrong-left-right emotional warfare that I couldn't get off and now I was dizzy, and things didn't make sense.

I found myself in a relationship with another narcissistic man, (the same one whose couch I was sitting on in that last flashback). He was also an alcoholic, coming fresh off a divorce and a mediocre acceptance that he waited too long to join the armed forces and living his only option as a member of the National Guard in Tennessee. We fell madly in love; he was from California, a few years older, wore skinny jeans and Vans, and I was IN HEAVEN.

He also drank like a fish and supported nonstop drinking. Most of our relationship was based on drinking. Bottles or boxes of my favorite wine every night, or a night of knock-down binge drinking at our favorite bar. I was the happiest when I was drunk.

Blind to the glaring red flags everyone warned me about, he fulfilled my need of having someone who reminded me of growing up and having that connection to familiarity I was so desperately missing. We bonded on California similarities and going to punk rock shows as teenagers. I saw him as my happily ever after.

Slowly his true colors emerged mixed with my endless lack of self-worth and no self-esteem. I dug and dug and dug into his past until I found something upsetting enough I could use against him as if he cheated on me, and used it to play on my insecurities to act in a manner that begged for constant reassurance. He was trying to make up for living a life that he felt he had wasted.

He was extremely demanding sexually. Soon it became a pattern: come home from work, get extremely drunk, allow him to fuck me. I don't even know how he enjoyed it half the time. We were in missionary, and I laid there still and cried. If I ever refused to have sex, I was told to sleep on the couch in the living room. I fell deep into a depression; partly because the alcohol had escalated so severely that I was completely numb emotionally. I don't even know if I had genuine emotions anymore. We both played out our insecurities and damaged self-esteems as if we were in the world's worst game of tug-of-war.

Our relationship became completely centered on sex. I didn't want to be there, yet I couldn't stand the thought of yet ANOTHER relationship being broken; I truly believe he felt the same way. My obsession of being "us" led to constantly pressuring him to propose and to tell me he was committed to spending his life with me. The next day I would withdraw and become offended and sensitive to everything he would say and do or accuse him of wanting someone other than me. To be very honest with you, it felt like it. This man arrived home one day with over $200 in trashy lingerie for me to wear and dress up. I was so confused.

He started introducing the idea of me having sex with another woman while he watched; he researched sex clubs for us to attend. I came into the habit of addressing him as "Sir" at all times and telling him I would do anything to please him.

One day he sent me a text with a list of sexual acts I needed to complete with/for him in order for him to stay in the relationship. I already had an unhealthy view of sexuality from things that I had been through.

It escalated to him attending a strip club regularly. He went every night or every other night. Finally, I said, "Let's go together. I'll go with you, and we can do this together," therefore condoning this behavior. So, we got drunk and went to the strip club. He bought me many lap dances, and the strippers flirted with him because they knew him.

At one point I went to the restroom, came back, and he was gone. I tried calling and texting him while looking around the club and I couldn't find him–for almost an hour. Going outside to get in the car, I forgot he had the keys, so I sat on the ground on the side of the strip club crying and trying to figure out what to do. He finally showed up and screamed at me asking why I left and why I was bothering him. Evidently, he was getting a private show from one stripper because I "stole his girl" from him in the club. *WHAT?!?!*

All I knew was I started swinging, repeatedly punching him in the face, anywhere I could hit him. He forced me into the car, and we drove off headed home, both so drunk I don't know how we made it home alive. The entire trip home was spent with me screaming, crying, and hitting him, giving him a black eye and a fat lip.

Finally, I was so tired from hitting him and crying I opened my car door on Interstate 40 and attempted to throw myself out of the car. He caught me before I fell out of the car and pulled me back in. I shut the door and pulled myself into a ball and cried. The next morning, we woke up; I was on the couch and he was in the bed. He had no memory of the previous evening and was wondering why I wasn't in bed with him. He asked me to come to bed. I did. We laid there in each other's arms like nothing had ever happened.

How did I get here? In all honesty, I don't know that I cared anymore.

I ended up leaving him eventually, more like it became so escalated he kicked me out of the apartment and threatened to have me evicted if I didn't leave. He stayed out all night and slept with strippers so, I concluded that it really was time for me to go.

My drinking got worse. I was "happier." Friends (fellow alcoholics) surrounded me, and I went back to my "dream job". Reality was, I drank enough to forget but not enough to remember how horrible my place in life was.

In a desperate measure, I turned to God. *Big surprise, right?* I had spent almost five years reading books, believing in crystals, going to therapy sessions and nothing was changing. My alcoholic roommate/ boss had made me watch church with her online. The search for something to fix me so I reverted back to God in a PTSD moment. It seemed the only thing that could fix me and was also the reason I was so fucked up. It was the piece missing from my life since I lost my family. I took a deep dive into a non-denominational church and contacted the pastor from my local location asking him to meet me. After I unloaded all my trauma, I asked him to help me; but he never helped me the way I wanted. I think I was expecting some sort of holy moment where he would lay hands on me, and I would be healed. He listened, offered support, told me to get involved, and take it one day at a time.

So I did. I immediately volunteered to help with church services on Sundays, standing in the lobby and welcoming people inside. I paired this with my non-stop drinking. Drinking every night and all weekend then showing up to church I'm SURE smelling like all the alcohol in Nashville. After church, my friend and I would go to a restaurant in the same parking lot and drink the rest of the day. This continued until my drinking had escalated again and I was too hungover to volunteer. I stopped showing up.

I met a man, whom I had an intense intellectual attraction to. Our sense of humor and personalities worked so incredibly well together. He repeatedly asked to date me, and I told him no. Trying to recover from a horribly abusive relationship made me no good to be with. We carried on as if we were in a relationship.

More in private than public. I spent five out of seven days and nights with him, but we showed no public affection, even on car rides alone he would try to hold my hand and I would refuse. However, alone in his bedroom we were in love. Keeping him at THREE arm's lengths away was my way of dealing with thoughts about what a horrible person I was, how useless I was, or how could anyone ever love me. I hated myself so much I did not care. Personal safety and self-respect were non-existent.

I would drink till I blacked out; there were many nights I didn't even remember large sections of time or even how I got home. Wake up and drink again. Drink at work, come home, go to the bar, and I'd somehow make it home. I was having the time of my life. My friends enabled my bad habits. I was never alone thanks to the man who was so enamored with me, yet I didn't have to admit any type of relationship to myself or him.

Vacationing in Portland, Oregon, I visited a friend; a man I had slept with in the past who I had always had a connection with, and undoubtedly used me for such.

Portland was beautiful. I could step outside my life back home for the eight days. Dive bars, wineries, breweries, sex, and watching movies in his loft. No one knew me and there I was, this mysterious woman garnering all the attention when we were out. It's crazy how you feel you can actually run away from your problems, a change of scenery clicking a reboot on your brain like a computer. You are not you anymore; no one knows you and it's beautiful. The me that was reality was on a shelf gathering dust for eight days waiting to be picked up, dusted off, and opened to all the pages falling out.

Drunk one night, that man back home texted me, and finally said he missed me and couldn't wait for me to come back. I immediately realized he was attached to me; he had feelings. I was going to RUIN HIM, I didn't want this. *How quickly can I end this? How can I hurt him so badly he will leave?*

"I slept with my friend."

He refused to speak to me. I tried and tried and tried. When I came back, instead of being relieved, it became a situation where I relived the trauma and pain from my family. I did something "wrong", and I was disposable and there was no understanding, no forgiveness.

My drinking escalated and became partnered with angry and depressing texts to this man, demeaning him and telling him off for not being OK with what I did or forgiving me. This paired with becoming infatuated with winning this man's favor as if I needed it to be normal again. In reality, I was acting out what I would ideally want to do with my family. I couldn't win them back so I would get satisfaction through having the approval of this man.

On top of that, I became more reckless with my drinking and decision making. I blew off mandatory work meetings and good friends; everything centered on alcohol. I had intense and brutal panic attacks at work and fits of crying, unable to calm down. I shared this with my manager (and soon-to-be close friend) and I didn't know what else to do but to keep drinking. I confided that my mental state was poor, and I didn't know where to go from there. Lying to almost everyone about what I was doing and why, when, and how, I became physical with many people when I was drunk. Becoming obsessed with having and being in a relationship. As if that would fix everything. I found myself in the worst depressive episode to date.

Down spiraling into a deep depression and wishing to die, I loosely began seeing a therapist a few months before but felt it wasn't really helping. I used men. I had no regard for anyone else's feelings.

This led me to one of my worst decisions; I was going to kill myself. I hit rock bottom; I was miserable. My ex-boyfriend had a new girlfriend, this man I was sleeping with and spending all of my time with hated me. I felt like no one loved me and I didn't deserve it even if they did. It was the equivalent of losing my family and children every time someone decided I wasn't good enough.

These scenarios played out many times with as many people, stupidly thinking perhaps if one of these worked out, it would take the place of what happened with my family. That would never happen. Instead, since I wasn't taking the time to heal from my many traumas, I repeated them over and over again with the same endings and creating a never-ending cycle of pain and hurt.

I laid out the pills in my hand and stared at them; I uncapped the alcohol. This was it. This was the only option I had. At that exact moment, a friend texted me and randomly invited me over insisting I come. I stepped away from the pills, grabbed the bottle, and went to his apartment. We stayed up all night watching reality competition shows and laughing. I did not speak a word of my plans but somehow this night changed my life. I came to the realization:

I had to stop drinking.

Going to his apartment was the universe or maybe God's way of telling me or showing me that killing myself wasn't the answer. When I got home the next morning, I blew off work; I logged on to our system and moved all my clients to other people. I never showed up and told no one; I wasn't going to.

A few hours later, the manager and the owner both texted me asking where I was and why I wasn't at work. Shortly after that the owner (also still my roommate) texted me, firing me. I didn't care at all. Apparently, my manager took it as a sign paired with my confession days before and alerted the owner that I was not in a stable state of mind. She was worried I would or had hurt myself. The owner quickly retracted firing me and told me if I didn't respond she would send the police to check on me.

The next part I don't quite remember; I know I still had a job, but I was off for a while. In my bedroom alone, I detoxed off alcohol. I laid in bed for days in a depressive stupor unaware of what my next move would be. All I knew of was this is what I had to do; the drinking had to stop.

I became an insomniac. My ability to fall asleep without alcohol was impossible. I would sleep four to five hours a night. My ability to function became difficult. A week passed, and I felt like now was the time to let my closest friends know what I had decided. I was going to be sober.

The first response I received from my closest friend at the time was, "Well that's the stupidest thing I've ever heard."

Was it? Was I just imagining a problem? Was I just trying to get attention? It's possible. But I was on this weird high from being sober and wanted it to continue. Shortly after this, I started attending AA and NA meetings with a coworker. She was in the middle of her 90 in 90 after coming off a stint in rehab (a stint we forced her hand in as an employee and noticing she was using drugs again). I had confided in her I decided to be sober, and she immediately told me to come with her.

I will never forget my first meeting, a CA meeting (Cocaine Anonymous–I had never tried that, but they explained it to me I didn't need to have done that to attend–I just needed to be an addict). Upon hearing the stories from other addicts, I immediately felt like I was not alone, and someone here understood me. I had been searching for this type of connection for years and it was here all along within the four walls of an addiction meetup.

I saw my therapist again, becoming obsessed with meetings. The obsession solidified the same woman who had introduced me to meetings sold me on the idea hot single guys filled these meetings (double win for me; I had truly scored).

Slowly but surely my relationship with my roommate/boss dwindled. It had fallen apart once; she treated me the same as all the men before her, just without the sexual control and abuse. The fact she was female, and this was strictly a friendship so enamored me; I never realized I could have been under the control of a narcissistic woman in this scenario. I think she found joy preying on weak women to control; she enjoyed her God complex.

She was angry with me for getting sober or so I believed, seeing a strength in me she wanted for herself and saw me bettering my life, and she didn't have the power to. She distanced herself from me and came down on me about my work ethic and performance. It grew to making our work life very uncomfortable and then she decided me living with her was an issue, raising my rent 200% overnight. It forced my hand to move out.

Feeling stronger than ever, I attended meetings six times a week and oddly enough most support came from all the friends I had made at the bar that I had been frequenting. They completely supported my sobriety and encouraged me every day. I know it sounds crazy but, not one person in that bar would serve me nor let me have a drink of theirs. They were so entirely strict about it; this was really the safest place for me to be at the moment. If I wanted to drink, it sure as hell wasn't happening there and I had the feeling of community and family. They also still liked me just as much even though I was sober.

Eventually, my work life became extremely uncomfortable. People were lying about my behavior and things I had said. Pulling me into a one-on-one meeting with my manager, I was questioned about everything; I had to deny the horrible rumors. Realizing my manager and I were not the friends I thought we once were led me to a wrongful demotion at my job. I was in such shock but also realized that this environment was detrimental to my continued healing, so I walked out and never turned back.

Driving home from the salon that day, I received an email from the volunteer leader at the church I had attended; remember, the one I did a deep dive into thinking it would fix me by simply volunteering and when it didn't immediately work, I abandoned the responsibility so I could go drinking. He proposed an offer to meetup and talk. Realizing I had been missing, he wanted to reach out to see how I was. I took this as God's blessing and His hand in showing me the right path to be on at this point in my life. To this day, I still believe this. It left me curious to find that out. Taking him up on his offer, we met at a local coffee shop, and I unloaded everything on him.

I think this was the first time I was really vulnerable with a stranger. We knew little about each other. The power I felt from sharing my story in strength and not always weakness was something I had not experienced before. I always relayed my life in ways of pain and sorrow for sympathy and empathy, for someone to commiserate with me.

Sharing with him honestly, I admitted my struggles and traumas, yet taking responsibility for the actions that had ensued in my life by the hands of my decisions. Sharing my desire to make a change completely with myself. Little did I know or realize this was the beginning of one of the most influential friendships of my life.

I started volunteering again, the immediate community I gained there filled a lot of holes that were open in my heart and soul. I had put myself in a frame of mind that my attempt to draw closer to God never worked before or was an option because I still had the idea that God was the version I grew up believing; this strong judgmental scary force that would never approve of me or who I was as a person. All these years since I have now been gone, I never spoke badly of the Jehovah's Witnesses other than it caused my family to disown me which I laid complete blame on the Organization (and still do) and never spoke badly of God. If it ever came up, I would always say, "God is just not for me but good for you." Once I realized I had to let go of that version of Him and start from scratch my entire world and eyes opened for the better.

I was open-minded to the idea of a God and what He could do and be for me. It excited me to learn about God and His people in a church and under a roof that whatever I looked like and whatever I did was OK. This church believed the same. I never imagined that the God out there WOULD be OK with this. I started immersing myself 100% into church activities, 100% into AA meetings, and 100% into going to the gym.

The combination of these three things would be what FIXES ME. Looking back I wasn't even really into any of these things whole-heartedly; I was into them because I thought that's what would FIX IT ALL. I was always a very black and white, one-track thinking, hyper fixated on things, all-in type of situation person. I always came up with an idea to "fix" everything and did it to a T. Healing Crystals. Therapy. Self-help books. Yoga. Becoming Sober. Trying to find God.

I could never really do anything at a decent rate, or balanced way. Everything was and is always an extreme manner for me. I felt like I was in the best place of my life I had ever been. My friendships were flourishing; I had all this amazing support being me and I was feeling actually loved again.

I decided to get baptized; dedicate my life to God, and rid myself of all the sins I committed before, in order to have a clean slate in His eyes and for myself as well. This did wonders for me, reveling in the feeling that drawing close to God, as I now understood Him, was saving me eternally and forgiving me of my sins. This was beautiful and amazing, and I believed in every part. I had such clarity of mind from becoming sober that I could understand and feel peace in the fact that no one really knew if it was all true, this God stuff. *But was it much different than believing in crystals and yoga and therapy and self-help books? Was it the fact that I believed in a water immersion as a symbolic washing of sins a traumatic indoctrinated thought?* No.

The choice was mine, and I was welcome and fully involved in the church, regardless. No one ever asked me to do it or told me I had to. EVER. I did it to help myself more than show an allegiance to God. I put on the frame of mind that this baptism was me relieving MYSELF of the bonds of shame and guilt. It was ME allowing myself the grace and moment to let go to move forward. Developing a relationship with God and what it means to me IS REAL. I don't write or convey any of this lightly in the sense of "well, here's another thing I thought would fix it".

For this moment in time, it did. I have nothing negative to say about it, at all. The people I met inside those walls were wonderful and still in my life to this day. I do still believe God loves me after spending thirty years of my life thinking he hated me.

Do I believe everything this church proclaims? No. *Do I agree with everything the Bible says?* No. *Do I think everyone inside the church is a good person?* No. But it brought me the peace and healing I needed and to be honest, out of all the things I chose to try to get this feeling, this one was probably the healthiest. I know that a lot of it was where I was spending my time and my focus was in better areas and directions. But mostly, accepting a religion again, or a relationship with God, allowed me the moments to find MYSELF AGAIN, and that's all I needed it for. *Do I think I have to be all in for it to save me and make me better?* NO.

My relationship with God and religion is just that, mine. I know a lot of us having left the Org are agnostic or atheist and OK great, fine; that's your life. I don't judge their experiences and words, that's their journey, just as this journey choice I have made shouldn't be theirs either.

I was wildly respected and loved here, and I wasn't pretending to be anyone else. I was myself. My personality, my sense of humor, my actions. I led a group of people ages twenty-five to thirty-five, along with my new friend, and I shared with them the things I had been through and listened to what they had been through.

Even though we were within the four walls of this church, once the conversations started there was very little God spoken of. It was people searching for connection, and for an ear to listen, simply having someone THERE. I took more from that than I did God in that moment.

I grew close with the youth there as well. My new nickname was "Church Mom" since I helped in the youth ministry and teenagers flocked to me for advice and someone to talk to. Struggling as teenagers do with identity and being accepted by their parents was something I could relate to, and they saw that.

I couldn't say this was entirely healthy. Obviously, this presence in my life fed a deep loss and insecurity in me, but goddamn was that so wrong? *Was I not allowed THIS?* Not everything is always as it seems and always so easy to say and this isn't OK, actually it was pretty sad and harmful. Maybe. Maybe not. To me it was a reminder I didn't need to feel ashamed to admit I was a mother.

Since I lost my children, I seldom spoke of them except to those very close to me because I did not want to face questions about them, people asking for pictures of what they look like, etc. These moments gave me the confidence again to accept and own that I AM A MOTHER, that I don't have to be ashamed of admitting this. I don't have to hide this side of me which is a huge part of who I am. It's beautiful, so beautiful, and for far too long, I had allowed the things of the past and the actions of my family and this organization to continually steal so much from me. Enough was enough.

This led to me wanting to help other Ex-Jehovah's witnesses heal from their trauma as I had healed from mine, or so it had seemed at the time. I created a non-profit organization that gave mental health help and referrals to further encourage and provide healing to move forward. Another avenue to deep dive myself into 100% and further distract myself from my healing that hadn't fully happened or addressed, although done innocently. I was desperately sharing what I knew and felt with others, to help them get to the place I was as well.

I remember the first time a year or two before; I had watched *Leah Remini: Scientology and the Aftermath*. Others had recommended it to me, it was the first popularized "cult" series garnering a lot of attention and waking people up to the realization that these things existed. About halfway through my very first episode, I had to turn it off. It was so incredibly reminiscent of what I had endured, it was terrifying. In this moment, it should have been a relief and bring comfort, but it was scary. It was all my deepest fears, insecurities, and pain in a moving picture. A few days later, I tried again and this time it was an overwhelming sense of comfort with the pain. I cried for the people in those stories and empathized with their pain. It also showed me that for once, I was truly not alone. That even though it was a different religion, it was the same outcome, the same traumas, the same pain. It was real and deep and honest and it was true.

In wanting to help others I thought of this show and what they did, and I wanted to do this as well but for those leaving the Jehovah's Witness Organization. I started indulging and deep diving into the community of Ex-Jehovah's Witness on Facebook as that is where I had found the largest community of them.

Definitely the most comforting part of the experience was meeting others who had been through almost identical situations with losing their family and children. It was in this moment I realized I had closed myself off from discovering this connection and finding others who truly related and instead spent years suffering alone and in silence. Then again, I think if this situation had happened before I became sober, I would not have been as receptive or seen it in the same light. I was open–heart and arms–accepting the fact that things that should have unfolded years ago to assist in my healing, were unfolding now as I was in a clearer state of mind to accept and process them.

My journey changed again; there was a plethora of broken people and very few people stepping in and stepping up to help them try to make a change. I was sober and healed so it was clear to me I would step in and fix all of them.

In reality, I ignored the road to continue my own healing and threw myself into other people's pain and "fixing them" instead of "fixing" myself. I quickly made connections; trauma bonding with others, thinking it was normal and healthy.

This turned into creating my non-profit, The Wounded Healers Foundation. Wide-eyed and motivated to make this the best thing that had ever happened to all Ex-Jehovah's Witnesses, I met a fellow survivor here in Nashville and we started promoting a meetup for other survivors to connect and exchange stories. (Regardless of how this came across, I do truly believe meeting other Ex Jehovah's Witnesses in person and connecting on that level is still a great tool in healing). A fellow survivor and I created content for our foundation, videos, thought-provoking conversations, positive thinking, anything to show there was life after the cult.

It became extremely frustrating when all these broken people weren't falling in line and healing. I spent all this time and invested in someone's story only for them to do absolutely nothing for themselves, but I was determined to continue.

Again, in reality, I ignored my own feelings and healing and focused on others. I dropped the alcohol and picked up the foundation I created and rationalized it healed and helped others.

I felt important and valuable. I struggled all these years feeling like I was worthless or never good enough; this narrative I created diminished those emotions. It caused me to become incredibly busy, which I enjoyed. The time spent with the foundation was worth the life-long connections I made.

I met two women from Canada who were getting the year they woke up from the cult tattooed on their body; I had bonded with them prior to this, and they encouraged me to do so as well. We figured out how to get our tattoos done at the same time. I showed up at the tattoo shop and shared with the artist the inspiration for my ink choice. After telling him my story, I saw his chest fall heavy; he expressed to me he was so honored to be a part of this moment.

The number 2018 was going to be tattooed on me. The other women had chosen spots on their bodies that resonated with them. I looked at my tattoo artist and said, "I want this on my ribs. I want it to be the worst pain I can feel." To me, the symbolism was more important than the ink. To have a permanent reminder of all the things that happened to me resulted from a horrible indoctrination. Looking down, it would remind me I had come out of the fog, and I opened my eyes to reality: the newfound grace that I could give myself, the answers for some of the ways I felt. I had this whole brand-new world before me as inspiration to keep growing.

It was a Sunday; I almost considered not attending church services that day. In fact, I had a friend later tell me he thought about telling me not to attend as well. To this day I don't remember what exactly the point of the message was, all I remember was the story involved this example: There was a man who came to church every week and saved a seat for his daughter who he was estranged from his life. As his relationship with God grew and he fixed things in his life, partnered with prayer, the relationship mended, and she eventually joined him in church.

Stories like these were only a tormenting reminder of the fact my experience of THAT kind of forgiveness had not happened and further fueled the feeling that it never would. I sat there and cried; the same tears I would cry every Mother's Day and every one of their birthdays. It was the deep realization this was still very much a reality for me.

There was a prayer card on each chair; they encouraged us to write our own prayer and post it on the lobby prayer wall. That day I wrote my most desperate of prayers, that God bring my children back to me.

As I walked out of the auditorium, my pastor stopped me and asked me to sit with him. Noticing from where he was standing on the stage that I was crying, he asked me what was on my card. I cried and told him the prayer and he asked for my card, and it would be the prayer he prayed. I obliged and felt hopeful that God would answer it. About a month after this my life changed forever, once again.

I found them.

I. FOUND. THEM.

Every once in a while, I searched for my kids on social media; only this time I came across my daughter's profile on Pinterest of all places. A few hours later I had discovered them both on Instagram.

Every part of my body had sunken and seemed to fall into my stomach. *Was this real? Had this happened?* My eyes fell on current pictures of them. I finally got to see what they looked like as young adults, a picture I only imagined for years and never knew if I was right or not. They looked the same yet completely different, and it put even more into perspective how much I had missed and how they were not the same children that I KNEW anymore.

Regardless of that, it left me pondering, had God ACTUALLY answered a prayer? Prayers worked?

The sheer terror of this moment actually happening combined with all the excitement, brought on a mixture of emotions I never knew existed in a human being; I did not know what to do with them. I began a kaleidoscope of moments in my mind for the next hours and replayed all of my favorite memories and moments with them, extremely painful things I blocked from my mind and the notion I did not deserve to enjoy those memories anymore.

It took me a day, but I finally reached out to my daughter first. She replied the next morning, in shock and with anger, but that slowly turned into sadness, and she lowered her initial wall. Telling me how desperately she had missed me and didn't know why I left.

My eyes floated over those words of hers a thousand times. Looking at them, I felt her pain. There were so many things running through my mind, so many feelings came back to me I had deadened being their mother and protector. And yet, looking at her pictures and feeling as if I was speaking to a stranger, feeling like a failure as a mother for even feeling that way.

It was enough to throw me into a tailspin of emotions I could not control. Tears flowed freely once again, the same tears I had cried for the last six years, and I still cry for them almost daily.

A strange yet familiar relationship via social media messaging started for us. After my daughter, I reached out to my son, and he reconnected as well.

There was extreme hesitation from us all, and footsteps of caution into the unknown. I was terrified of the things they would say and the things they were told. They were both extremely inquisitive about my version of the events that happened that led to our separation. I explained to them both the best I could; the moment I had been dreaming of for six years was here. As candidly as my vocabulary allowed, the events that led to me separating from them. It seemed as if they accepted what I said and comprehended it, whether they believed it remained to be seen.

This was the message I sent to my son:

"I am sorry, I am sorry for how all of this unfolded. It's not as simple as I just left. I did try to contact you and your sister numerous times and received no answering of the phone or no response. I did the best I could with the situation as it was. And I know that doesn't excuse the pain I've caused. And for that I will be forever sorry. But I have looked for you and your sister for all these years waiting for this moment to tell you I love you and I miss you and think about you every day of my life and hope you are doing so amazing and are so happy. I don't wish to cause you any upset. And I'm sorry if I have. I just have searched so long. And I'm here to talk if you want."

Upon unpacking the moment and the words I expressed, I received this response from my son:

"I know from everyone's standpoint, they're upset, confused, uneasy, etc. For myself I'm more so puzzled and confused more than anything. But I don't hold grudges and I'm willing to forgive even if there was nothing to necessarily to forgive in the first place. In the end, I don't expect you to just not be involved with us in any way at all, because it seems like you want to see us and you're sorry. So, I believe you want to go into action about it. **You shouldn't have to live your life hiding, especially from family."**

PART III

THE ROAD TO HEALING

The year started on a high note, I finally found my kids and slowly communicating more and more. I was sober, active, involved in my church and the youth ministry, and I ran a nonprofit that was changing lives. However, my own mental health had deteriorated; I was neglecting it but was convinced since everything happening was something I had always been waiting for, on paper, and was ideally what I was supposed to be doing, everything was OK.

The only thing missing was the man I hurt so badly, and I became obsessed with proving I was different and gaining his forgiveness. I groveled for a year and a half desperately attempting for this man's approval and acceptance that I was once again a good person. Listening to him tell me repeatedly that I hurt him, and he couldn't trust me, but then asking me to come over late at night to have sex because he said, "he was still extremely attracted to me." I obliged because I held this belief that sex could fix anything a man was upset about. *Did I want to?* No. *Did I do it because he wanted it and I thought it would fix this?* Absolutely.

In this moment of bliss where everything was going "right", I couldn't help but remember all my past relationships since I lost my kids. Every single one that was substantial enough, ended with them saying,

"If you actually try to get your children back, I would be with you again" or "Why aren't you trying to get them?" or "Maybe you wouldn't be so fucked up if you didn't lose your own kids, even they don't want you". To me, since I had found my children I thought, *this is it, this is the missing piece of myself I have found to show I am worth of being with him again.*

This turned into a never-ending physical and emotional merry-go-round ride neither of us ever wanted to be on, yet neither one of us could stop. I checked every box, and it was all going so well. The only thing missing was changing the narrative of what a romantic partner thought of me and how they accepted me. I gained "acceptance" of being worthy and of value in every other area of my life, except where he was concerned.

Eventually we found ourselves in an actual committed relationship. To this day I'm not sure why, I believe I had genuine feelings for him, but I also believe I had this driving desire that being in this relationship would complete "fixing" me. It would fill the void of the resolution with my family. It would also prove to me I was worthy and of value in a romantic relationship.

Now I'm not sure if I was in love with him or in love with the idea of what loving him, being forgiven, and loved by him would mean. Things were gradually unraveling for me mentally and I wasn't sure how to stop it. I was slowly but surely spiraling down into this deep depression; the heaviest black cloud I had experienced so far.

I created and accepted this narrative that becoming sober would "fix" everything. I threw myself into sobriety with a full and open heart. Attending meetings five to seven times a week, abstaining from alcohol, throwing myself into church services, and telling myself that doing these good things would put me in a better frame of mind, around better people; therefore, I would have better focus.

These beliefs were not all wrong. The wrong part comes from thinking that's all I had to do, that no work was needed on my part as far as addressing my trauma and processing feelings and emotions that had yet to be touched. In my mind, I had been in therapy for six years at this point, so I was good in that department.

But here I was, trudging through the worst year of my life. Or so I thought. I couldn't hold a job. I had learned there was a fibrous tissue/ tumor living in my jaw; it was unknown how or why it had even formed, but I had to have surgery to remove it.

I demanded approval from this man. I demanded to see my children. I demanded to have it all, perfectly, and it wasn't happening. I had no patience for work anymore. I was healed and fine, everything needed to fall in line.

Every time I tried to express my emotions, he met me with "that's not a normal reaction," which angered me like nothing else. How many times are people going to tell me that how I feel, *ISN'T NORMAL?*

WHY ARE MY EMOTIONS, OPINIONS, TRAINS OF THOUGHT NOT EVER NORMAL?

And the best one: *I AM SOBER. WHY ISN'T MY LIFE FIXED? WHY AM I NOT BETTER?*

I had surgery but there was nothing anyone could do for me to make me feel completely supported and loved. I had a breakdown at one point because I was about to go through this possibly life-altering surgery and experience and my family was nowhere to be found. In these powerful moments of life that could be life changing, I couldn't suppress the innate reaction to want to call my mom or dad, to lean on them and share the pain or the joy. It was a strong desire of wanting my family to care and be concerned and tell me it would all be OK. I had multiple people around me showing and pledging an allegiance to me which I had never experienced in my life from family and somehow it was still never enough. In my heart, I knew that no matter what I did or how much I healed I would forever chase the high of what I lost during the good times with my family.

Sadly, there was no one out there that replaced family and instead of making peace with that and accepting it, I lived in this period by chasing it in things I had dedicated and invested all of my time and effort into.

I had never felt so alone. I had lost my dream job. My man and I were fighting again. I was trying to recover from surgery on my jaw, but once again I was drowning in the feeling that I was doing everything right so why wasn't my world fixing itself.

I always struggled with feeling like those in my life had never and *would* never care about me in the right way. In my mind, I envisioned and had a feeling of what that looked like; it was a version of what I did for others. When it wasn't shown or given to me exactly as I would do for them, I convinced myself they didn't really love me. I was a fool this entire time thinking they were actually my friend, or it wasn't the exact friend I wanted that was showing it to me.

The one bright spot in these moments was I was going to California to see my children for the first time in six years; this got me through every day and kept me sober. The moment I had dreamed of for six years was coming and soon I would wrap my arms around them again and hold them. I could hear their voices. I could touch them. Everyone around me was so excited for me and I reveled in that excitement with them on the outside but inside my mind, I was losing it. I was falling deeper and deeper into a mental anguish I had no control over.

They refused to see me.

The night before I was leaving, I learned of this. I planned a two-week stay in California to see and spend time with them. I think I was in such disappointment and pain I went numb, and began the free fall into the poisonous prison I put myself in. It was the most dreadful flight and traveling experience I had ever experienced; it felt like I was walking straight into a fiery hell of my own decisions. It forced me to relive losing them all over again, flying to and staying in the same city where it had happened, and facing the consequences of what had happened and the result of them feeling hurt and abandoned by me.

I've always been good at compartmentalizing my emotions . . . clearly. I used alcohol to assist, but now I was sober, and it would embarrass me to relapse. All

I could imagine was the people who supported me wouldn't want anything to do with me anymore because I was a fuckup and unworthy.

The first thing I did once I got settled at my friend's house was to change clothes and go to the gym. I replaced drinking with another outlet: working out. I was determined to make good choices and do things other than drink. So, I went to the gym, worked out, and then went to another friend's house for dinner, surrounding myself with others, another sobriety tactic.

That next morning, the first thing I did was go to an AA meeting. To be honest, to this day it was probably the most influential AA meeting I have ever attended. It was nine other alcoholics and me, all men in their seventies to nineties (yes seriously). I could tell I stepped into a meeting that no one outside this circle ever attended. They welcomed me with open arms and showed so much excitement to have someone new attend. They asked me to open the meeting, and I explained to them I was sober almost a year at this point and gave a shortened version of all the events that led me here.

At this point, they each took turns uplifting me and sharing short stories of their own journeys, really focusing all their energy on making sure I did not relapse and making sure I felt supported and encouraged in not relapsing. It definitely uplifted me momentarily and gave me a power inside where I felt like, *damn I got this. I'm fine, this is fine, everything is fine.*

After leaving I drove around all the places I shared with my children: the places we used to live, the places we visited, where we lived our everyday lives.

Driving through the same familiar neighborhoods, I was searching for them in all those places and searching for myself as well. I had set off on a tour of a past life and the me I was before losing everything.

I drove by the restaurant where I saw them last. I stared, wanting to lovingly gaze upon that building with admiration and joy of all the meals we shared there, all the good times that echoed inside those walls and lived on the furniture we touched. Instead, all I saw were the images in my mind, the moving picture show of the last time I laid my eyes on them in person, walking away from me. How badly I wanted to be back in that moment.

That feeling of being uplifted and strengthened from that AA meeting by those unsuspecting men had vanished.

I couldn't bear it anymore. My friend's house where I was staying was in the exact neighborhood I raised the kids. Everything around me was so nostalgic and warm and at the same time, like a sharp dagger killing me more and more by the minute.

I left and went 100 miles east to Palm Springs; Brother lives here. I needed to leave these reminders and try to change how overwhelmed and upset I was. I tried to make the best of my time left by spending time with Brother and lying by the pool pretending everything was fine.

Crying myself to sleep and waking up every morning crying. Forcing myself to pretend that what just happened didn't happen, I tried to be positive and make the best of the situation.

After a week there, I traveled to Las Vegas to spend time with Desarae and her family. Pouring my heart out to her was always one of the world's best therapy sessions. The two weeks I spent out west were one huge distraction from reality. It sufficed in the moment but the nagging fact in the back of my mind, like a devil on my shoulder, was I wasn't on "vacation" forever. At some point I had to go home and accept this happened.

I threw myself into demanding comfort, reassurance, and attention from a man whom I was in the world's longest game of tug of war with. Those closest to me who had been there with me either before it all happened six years ago or had pivotally changed my life for the better since it all happened, surrounded me with support and love and kindness. Yet all I wanted was it to come from him and he wasn't giving me exactly how I wanted it. I went through the motions in real life and privately in conversations with him; I was desperate and volatile. It was as if I had no one else to take my frustration out on so we played out our own version of a tragedy and lived it out in real time. By the time I got home we were over once again.

Rock bottom looked a lot like living in the same pajamas for a week, barely eating, never showering, sleeping 75% of the day, and ignoring those reaching out to me to comfort me. All the pieces I had glued together shattered in the most dramatic way and the shards became so small they turned to dust and were swept away with the slamming of the door on this moment. I was in the strangest fog and haze I had ever experienced, but still sober, thankfully.

Looking back, I believe it was only because this was literally the only thing in my life I could control: my sobriety. I desperately grasped onto this lifeline as the last thing left that would keep me together and make everything right again, repeating as I always had by grasping onto something external for a radical cure.

I became fixated on how I looked, making myself beautiful would make me feel better. Looking back on pictures of this time, 70% of them were selfies of me, undoubtedly posting them on social media for approval and attention and to hide the fact that I was dying inside. I wanted to portray this strong woman idea I had served to everyone and sustain the idea of what they expected. This was not because of anything they had done or said, but from what I believed I had to do. I reached for anything to feed the part of me that was empty.

In the last year, I had grown even closer to my best friend in Nashville. She had a baby in May of that year. I became infatuated with her son; not in a "I'm going to steal your child and claim them as my own" type of way, but as, "This is my chance to change the narrative with a child and have them love me". Although I am not sure which one is worse. I believed a part of this was to prove to myself that I wasn't defunct of attachments with a small child, and it was something I had purposely kept myself from doing all these years. My relationship with this child became my new focus and all my attention went to him. I lived in this world of trying to make myself look as pretty as possible so I felt good about myself and spent as much time as I could with my new nephew to get him to love me. Truthfully in those moments it never felt that way; I found a peace in calmness in bonding with him. It gave me a sense of normalcy that this connection wasn't impossible for me.

My involvement and attention to God and church had become almost nonexistent. I didn't blame God for any of this, I really never had. In my mind, God had nothing to do with anything; He couldn't hurt or help me, so it made no sense for me to be angry with or blame Him. It was a sense of embarrassment and disappointment that kept me from going. I felt I had become a letdown to those within the church walls that looked up to me; they were so excited that I was going to see my children. Coming back in person meant I had to accept and confirm it didn't happen and so many people would be disappointed. I tried many times and every time I went inside, I just cried. The overwhelming sadness and pain I didn't even realize was happening caused the crying.

Looking back, I realized I attached the fact I had found my kids to becoming close to God. It wasn't a blame, rather it was an association. Therefore, it was the reason being in that building and being close to God again was so traumatizing to me. I also didn't feel worthy anymore; I'm sure that was also a moment of reverting to previous traumas and ideas of my value.

Slowly I functioned "normally" again. I celebrated my one-year sobriety, dramatically changed my appearance, and started hanging out with my friends more often and actually enjoying summer. In reality, I faked it, going through the emotions and finding enough things to distract myself from the deep and inner thoughts in my mind. Once again, I ignored my emotions and pushed them down. Although at this point I wasn't drinking; I was acting out the same unhealthy behaviors of avoidance in dealing with processing my genuine emotions. This wasn't "someone cut me off while I was driving upset", this was monumental trauma that repeated when I hadn't healed or dealt with it the first time. And again, I thought I was doing well, and I was safe because I was still sober.

This man and I got back together, I attended church again and was involved with Sunday Services and the Youth Ministry. Things in my life got better, seemingly. I got a job working at an addiction center trying to get people to commit to rehab. I felt like the idea was a good one though poorly executed.

Again, I grasped at something to fix what was broken; being sober fixed me so now I needed to fix others. What concluded from all of this was my environment projected onto me, I took it all personally and it fueled my disfunction. I became irritable and sensitive to everything and everyone because, in my mind, I knew best since I went through it. I lost that job, of course, as they deemed me "difficult" to work with. From there I thought, *I should work at a mental health hospital and go back to school for psychology.* I completely immersed myself in the clinical aspect of psychology and other people's problems shoving mine further and further down. *What problems?* I studied addiction and babysat patients in a mental health ward; I was the shining example of recovery and someone with their head on straight. *Who cared if I couldn't hold a job or a healthy relationship to save my life? Who cared that I tried to see my kids, and they rejected me?*

Instead of being able to handle bumps in the road properly I spiraled yet again down a deeper hole. In my mind, this was the best I was ever going to be so the way I handled all my trauma and discomfort was fine, a prime example of perfect mental health. In the meantime, I bounced back, was in a good place, and had it all together, in time my kids would come around. I hadn't bounced back from anything; I continued to overwhelm myself with enough things to distract myself successfully from the issues and the pain.

My good friend, coworker, and fellow Sister in Christ suddenly died. When I worked at the salon, we would talk all day at work and had formed a special friendship. Unspoken, but clear to us was the reason for our friendship. It heavily devastated me. Obviously, we were close in our own special way, and I was grieving the loss, but I also grieved the loss of my children along with her.

It sent me into the start of another downward spiral, once again sabotaging the romantic relationship I was in. I became closed off, hypersensitive, and defensive; it destroyed the relationship yet again between this man and me. As with every other time, not without fault of both parties, it ended. Depressed and alone, I worked twelve-hour shifts while trying to keep up with school.

That's when I started cutting.

I felt such an extreme loss of ways to release all the pent-up frustration and pain. Drinking wasn't an option, but I wanted something to distract me and take me away. I still didn't want people to be disappointed in me because if I disappointed them, they would discard me as my family did.

I bought razors and broke them to remove the blades, holding that blade in my hand and slicing the tops of my thighs was a relief. Like sobriety, I could control this act; I could forget about the pain inside for the moment because I focused on the physical pain I was inflicting. Skin picking, messing with cuts, causing them to break open free and bleed, causing myself physical pain was something I had practiced for some time. I loved the act of getting a tattoo, watching it penetrate my skin, and feeling the extreme pain was a sensation I enjoyed probably more than I should. Cutting was no different. The temporary relief was worth it to me.

One of my "Sisters" got married the month before. I helped her plan and took her for her first wedding dress shopping experience. I also took her then-fiancé to get his custom suit for the ceremony; picked it out and ordered it. I stood up for them at the altar her friends and family had made in the backyard and shed genuine tears of happiness for her. Sharing this time and moment with her and our other friends helped. They reminded me they were in my corner, and I had a family here if I wanted it.

A month later, one of our core friends from out west called me at work. It was a Tuesday morning. We talked every day but through text messages and only called each other when something was wrong; so, I knew right away things weren't right. I answered the phone, and she said "****** is dead". I dropped everything at work and got in my car and drove to my Sister's house.

When I arrived, I found her in the kitchen with our Gram. I didn't know what to do or say. That night many emotional things occurred, those of which are not my story to tell; they are hers, but it broke me. The next few days I took the lead planning his funeral to try to ease her pain. She refused to leave the house and could not handle what needed to be done. I planned it with his mom and stepdad, signing as the witness to consent for his cremation just as I signed as the witness on their marriage certificate a month before.

Selfishly I thought once the funeral was over: *What else could happen? Haven't I been through enough? After all the events that happened this year, now this? Why hadn't I been able to help?*

Internalizing every tragic moment that happened around me since I arrived back from trying to see my children; this event was no different. At this point, I began questioning God. After all I had done in drawing close to Him, getting baptized and dedicating my life to Him, He had slowly been robbing me of all my happiness and sanity little by little, one by one. I still didn't blame Him; I put it on my shoulders since I thought I deserved it because I wasn't good enough for Him to make it better.

It was at this point that I really thought and believed that it really was all a façade. I believed for years since my family threw me away that I was never special or treasured by anyone; no one ever REALLY loved me. I didn't REALLY have anyone around me physically that cared or wanted to be there for me. I was trash and useless and invaluable; no matter how hard I tried, I could never make things better.

I began to drink.

Driving home from work one night, I rationalized since I was off the next day, I could get drunk and forget everything that was weighing me down; I could just RELAX. After struggling over the past year with medications to help the depression and anxiety I was already going through for the past seven years, it clearly was not working and to be honest, when I was drunk, I felt great. I was relaxed and happy and carefree and smiled and had fun; at that moment, it was the only side of alcohol I remembered. Becoming numb to everything I was feeling inside was the only rational answer; I just wanted it all to STOP. I tried it all; I gave it a good go and led with all the healthy ways to handle all this madness and I was out of ways to try.

I stopped at a liquor store I had frequented many years ago that was out of the way in my town. I knew if I went there, I wouldn't run into anyone I knew. It had been some time since I was there so they would not remember me. I bought a 4-pack of Barefoot Pinot Grigio wine. Four little bottles. I think I did this to convince myself it was not a big deal and was not a lot. I drank all four that first night, equivalent to an entire bottle of wine.

I felt wonderful. Hungover, but wonderful.

Still secluding myself at home so no one would know, I was fun again. My sense of humor was on fire with my friends, although only through text messages. I was back to my old self, absolutely no inhibitions, and I was HAPPY; I felt happy. I did this for a few weeks, it quickly escalated to drinking every night even if I had to work the next day. Hiding it from all my friends, no one had any idea.

My mental state had taken a very sharp nosedive. What once was me feeling carefree again quickly turned into an enormously powerful and dangerous depression and self-loathing. I would not suggest working in a mental hospital when struggling with personal mental health issues. Yes, there was an aspect of going to work every day that I felt like, and I mean no offense by this, I was the most mentally well-balanced person. Not a great comparison if that is only true inside the walls of a mental health ward.

The days passed and soon it was November 20th.

I worked that day; I woke up at the usual time, 5am. Hungover. Got ready for work, drove to work, parked my car, went inside, and started my day as if nothing unusual was happening. I pretended to be my usual chipper self, laughing with my coworkers, and greeting all the patients.

On the inside, I was having the worst mental breakdown to date.

The walls of a mental health ward had a different smell from all the other walls in other buildings. The feeling you get from being a defective human being stings a little differently there as well.

All I wanted to do was get through this day, go home, and get drunk. As the day passed it turned into, go home, get drunk, and emerging thoughts of suicide grew.

Intense self-loathing and negative self-talk. Listing all the reasons I was useless and worthless. I was replaying what happened in court that day I lost my children. Replaying going to visit my kids and them rejecting me. Replaying my failed relationships, friendships. Reminiscing on the good times with my family and beating myself up for not being good enough to still be there enjoying them. Marinating my mind with how I was such a waste of life. Truth be told this was a familiar place to be mentally; I had lived in this mind space for years now and visited often.

The man I had been back and forth with for a year and a half, texted me. In frustration, he "yelled" at me his opinions about: why I couldn't get it together, why I always left, why I always panicked, why I always acted like everyone was out to get me, why I always thought things and viewed things so completely different from what was "normal". Basically, sending over in written form, letters for me to read repeatedly that confirmed all the horrible things I already thought about myself. I know he didn't know my state of mind now. It really showed me how you never know what someone is going through so always be careful about what you say. I remember asking him to stop, that I was having a bad day.

In this moment, after reading his words, I decided I would go home after work and end my life.

On the drive home that night from work, I felt at peace. A strange calmness enveloped my body in my decision, there was no clarity regarding the sheer mistake and tragic reality of this moment in my mind.

I hesitate to list details here; I don't feel it serves a purpose. Anyone who has been in this place mentally, knows what this moment looks like, feels like, and smells like. Those who haven't felt this way, I hesitate to believe would ever understand or accept how one could get here logically or how any of this is rational.

I could only describe it as all the broken pieces become shards inside of you and the pain and discomfort of living became so overwhelming that I only wanted peace.

I know what brought me to this moment, and I read accounts of many others who had been here as well. Very often it was not even about wanting to be dead; it was about wanting all the pain, discomfort, instability, failed relationships, inability to cope, unable to feel, unable to be "normal", unable to explain correctly what's going on, the inability for ANYONE to understand you . . . to cease. I didn't believe I really wanted to die, I wanted everything as I knew it to end.

So, I gave it my best shot.

The next morning came. Meaning, I never expected there to be one.

I briefly remembered the night before. I talked with this guy I attended church with and made some sort of comment about I'll call or text him the next day if I'm still here; he called me freaking out, and I promised him I would be fine . . . that was after I sent him the nude pics he wanted. Here I was, trying to die yet still trying to get some sort of validation one more time from someone. *Unbelievable.*

The memory of that day is still hazy, I am not even sure if I left the house. Or showered. Or ate. I remember a friend of mine reaching out or I reached out to her; it wasn't completely uncommon since we spoke frequently.

She suffered from Suicidal Ideation (SI) and mental health issues as well. I ended up sharing with her what happened the night before and she was adamant about taking me to the hospital.

I think I agreed to go to appease her, to go to the hospital and have them tell us I was fine. I also didn't care, I wanted to disappear somewhere and not see anyone or talk to anyone for a while. I clearly was not of a rational mind. Or maybe there was a part deep down inside me giving its best attempt at asking for help. *Who knows what all the thoughts were I had at this time?*

I got to the hospital and went into the ER; they brought me into triage which was a private room and I just lost it. Never have I been in a deeper state of desperation and brokenness. My desire to no longer be alive was detailed to the nurse. I was done with living. I didn't care anymore. They took me to a private room in the ER, gave me a sedative, and told me it was policy for a police officer to sit outside my door to monitor me.

I thought, W*ow, this just gets better and better. Could you fuck up ANY MORE THAN THIS?* No grace and understanding for myself, instead instant judgment and picking myself apart, tearing myself down. *You couldn't* *even kill yourself properly; now you're in a hospital and a police officer had to watch you. GOOD JOB.*

They woke me up at 3am, informing me that an ambulance transport would take me to an inpatient mental health facility. I was so out of it. I remember little; at one point, I looked out the back window of the ambulance and saw other cars on the freeway. My mind drifted to the headlights of the cars behind me, a stark black night with lights chasing me as if they were supporting me or trying to reach me to help. But here I was in the back of this ambulance that was carrying me away from them.

Looking back on this moment I secretly wished for those headlights to be my family, rushing to me. Instead, they were headlights of a person on their way to work or on their way back from living their day; looking back at me through the door windows, they probably wondered how I ended up there.

I arrived in the middle of the night; they took my vitals, gave me some more sedatives, and showed me my room. I fell asleep immediately.

The next morning, I woke up in a room. A cot with a foam mattress, a pillow, one blanket, and a roommate in the bed next to me; there was a bathroom in our room with a foam flap door.

They took all my personal effects. The clothes on my person were all I had. Geographically, I had absolutely NO IDEA where I was. I came out of my room, and I got some juice, more meds, and then went back to the room and back to sleep. This continued for the rest of the day. I don't think I ate. A nurse came in my room and gave me meds instead of me having to wake up and leave my room. To this day, I don't know how long this routine actually lasted; maybe just that first day? Eventually the nurses told me I had to come out of the room, eat when everyone else ate, and come out for the classes they provided at different times during the day.

I sat there in a trance-like state staring at the ground without blinking. Here I was, in an establishment that was basically the same type of place I worked at. How. Did. This. Happen. More tears. More crying. More desperation.

In the beginning of this mess, they informed me I was there on a psych hold for at least five days in a co-occurring unit. I explained to them it had been a long time since I felt like a medication worked for me; I was in a state of constant anxiety that only progressed and deepened every day.

The first two psychiatric nurse practitioners I saw, didn't seem to hear anything I was saying. I talked, but they were busy already prescribing the typical cocktail everyone else in this ward received. This only added to the frustration I was having. *What in the world would this accomplish?*

Most of the nurses and care coordinators were very nice. There was one man in particular who really took me under his wing like a father. He sat and talked to me about God, drinking, the decisions I'd made, and the ones I needed to make. He prayed with me and for me, even bringing me a Recovery Bible to read and take in God's Word while I was trying to figure out what to do or what needed to be done.

The day classes were extremely annoying and mundane; "Write something that makes you happy and then color it and then implement it perfectly into your life, so you never commit suicide or use drugs and alcohol ever again."

The work of a mental health facility is not being downplayed or undermined by me; I am only expressing how it felt from the standpoint of someone in a very fragile mental state. Drugs seemed to be the only thing that could fix me; I felt like I had exhausted everything else. Therapies, self-help books, church, these stupid worksheets that made me feel like I was in third grade again (and they literally gave you a giant box of crayons as writing instruments). These were the focus of my time there BUT having access to an adult book on the preferred reading list or the top ten books to read related to trauma or C-PTSD to read and study was prohibited. Literally.

I finally could meet with a Nurse Practitioner (NP) who listened to me after complaining for days that I felt no one was listening. It was determined the first step was to get me regulated on a proper medication regime; I was not on one for the past forever years that I felt ever worked. We experimented with many combinations and dosages. Some I felt a little better on and some I felt worse; it was very frustrating. But I appreciated that someone was taking the time to do this with me instead of the initial, "OK take this now and we are done".

I relaxed, and my moods improved because of the validation I received. I made friends with other people in my ward, again, trauma bonding. Being social and making friends took me to another place mentally, and it was like nothing was ever wrong in the first place, which is probably how I got here to begin with. I think that, partnered with the fact I was away from everything being locked in here. I had no responsibilities, and no one knew where I was and what was wrong; it was like I could disappear completely.

At this point I decided rehab was the best option. I was a raging alcoholic; I couldn't be trusted. I had to go somewhere to fix my alcoholism. Again, I searched and placed blame on anything other than the root of these problems. I set my heart on rehab being the one thing that would "fix" me: same as all the other things before. A girl and I became friends in the hospital and made a pact to go to the same place (FYI: making a pact in a mental health hospital and making friends there was REALLY not a solid move).

Not only this, I met a man in there and was convinced we were meant to be; funny that we met in a mental health ward (also not a good idea). My focus shifted from myself and my healing and well-being to gaining the admiration and acceptance from this man. We exchanged numbers since he was getting out before me, and we were insistent on pursuing this as a relationship. Even while writing this, I realized how completely insane that was. I told no one about him because I knew it was an absolutely horrible idea, but at that time, I craved the attention from a man.

Eleven days I spent there, and to be honest, the idea of leaving wasn't entirely wonderful. I regulated myself into this protective bubble where I didn't have to admit or address to the outside world what was happening. I could escape to this alternate life where no one even knew me, and I could start over in a way.

During this time, a new coworker at my job realized I wasn't at work and couldn't get a hold of me; she filed a missing person's report against me. Slowly I would come to learn that the police visited all my known residences in Nashville, my current home, and then the homes of the narcissistic ex-employer and the ex who I had shared that traumatic car fight with after the strip club. It had reached as far as being posted all over Facebook within Nashville groups saying, "Missing Person have you seen her?" So now, everyone CLEARLY knew. What an embarrassment. What an absolute embarrassing moment. *Could I stay here forever now? No? OK.*

When I finally left, I had missed 100 text messages on my phone and several voicemails. My immediate realization of this made me panic. I was not ready, nor could I hide anymore. I couldn't wait to get back to rehab. My best friend picked me up from the facility and took me home. I packed and handled some bills, things that needed to be done since I was the only person in charge of all that was me.

One of my friends from work (the same one who filed the police report), picked me up and took me to rehab. The instant relief I felt arriving there meant I could hide again and maybe people would forget about what happened with me, forget that something was wrong and move on to the next tidbit of heavy gossip. I also wanted the protection. I didn't feel safe with myself, and this seemed the best option.

God, get me out of this place.

Never in a thousand years had I ever pictured myself here. Immediately I was uncomfortable. Have you ever seen a shitty rehab in the movies where it's just dirty and old and over-populated? That's where I landed. I was terrified for my safety more than anything. They went through all my belongings and gave me half of them in a large black trash bag and stole what remained. My friend from the hospital arrived there two days earlier and was threatened physically by one of the other women in her cabin. IS THIS REHAB? Seriously? This was what was happening.

I had already detoxed in the hospital, so I going to stay in detox only overnight. They told me things and went back on their word, for instance: I was going to a cabin of general population then it never happened, asked if I had self-harmed before and when I said "Yes," ALL THE SUDDEN I had to stay in detox longer. Imagine standing before these people in a higher position, being ordered to take off my clothes to show them my scars; "Well, you have a history of being a cutter, in fact, take your clothes off so we can see." I literally stood naked in an office with two people staring at me while I asked them to explain why I had to stay in detox longer. I don't think I need to explain the absolute humiliation of that moment and lack of consideration to be treated like a human being.

Finding someone with compassion in this place was impossible. For those who are unaware, detox is where these facilities get most of their money. So, keeping me in detox was more about the money than me actually needing to be there. I was done; I asked to be released to go to another facility. Honestly, I'm surprised I still had a desire to go somewhere else but the thought of going home was worse.

When you ask to go home (drug and alcohol rehab facilities are at will), they bring some patients that have been there almost the entire thirty to ninety days to talk you out of leaving. They tried tactics of reminding me how bad an addict I was and how the most important thing was for me to stay there. As soon as the counselor and representative of the facility left the room, they looked at me and said, "Man this is fucked up. If I were you, I would leave too."

I called my sister from church and asked her to come get me. They took me to the front of the rehab and left me outside to wait for my ride in twenty-degree weather, literally on the street in the dark, with all my belongings still in that same trash bag with all my empty luggage.

The next day I arrived at Cumberland Heights, this time I drove myself. The registration and intake process were long but harmless and smooth (The intake nurse was a very attractive male. Yes, I understand this is a HUGE issue for me). The condition of the facility and the way they treated me were as different as night and day from the last one; it was beautiful. The women's cabin was two to a room, and the rooms were so big it was like staying in a really nice Hampton Inn hotel. Now THIS was more like it. Very few women, I think there were maybe ten or twelve when I first got there.

I was met with compassion and understanding by those who had been in my shoes before and had complete transparency in sharing it with me, explaining how they were no better than I. Facing the reality that I was here for thirty days, I was completely fine with that, anything to hide myself again.

I made friends quickly and settled in, learned the routine of how to find my classes, when it was time to eat and time for meds, and learned how to get away with being late to classes because I wanted to smoke more. Imagine the best summer camp for adults except you all have massive trauma and horrible coping skills.

My roommate and I came a day apart from each other and I truly believe this was one of the few reasons I stayed. Alcohol was our drug of choice (DOC), and we were both young mothers with older children. We even had a very similar sense of humor. We leaned on each other in these times, when I was weak, she was strong and vice versa, never hesitating to do what we could for each other. There was a strange comfort and unspoken support of spending time with so many other messed up people; it took the embarrassment away and made me feel like I was CLEARLY not the only one here with this problem. Literally everyone here was in the same boat.

But I still cried all the time and was suicidal. The anxiety took over, and I was miserable. I hated my counselor; she practiced very tough love and made me feel like my feelings were stupid and not validated. The supervisors came in and went through all my things and took anything that could remotely become a weapon. I felt violated and embarrassed. I spent a couple nights crying so hard they took me to the medical building because I was so overwhelmed with anxiety and wanting to die; all they would say to me was, "Just go back to your room and try not to think about it."

I struggled with feeling validated by anyone in a position of authority. Feeling like though I was expressing my thoughts and emotions, they shoved everything to the wayside. I felt overlooked. Every Sunday was family day and everyone's families and loved ones would come to visit and no one would show up for me. They even had family therapy, and I refused to attend. I had NO ONE.

I tried again to help myself and everything around me was screaming, letting me know once again that I wasn't worth it. In extreme desperation, I attempted to contact my father and see if he would speak to me. I called him three times in a row and no answer, so I finally left him a voicemail with my cell phone number saying it was me and I wanted to speak to him. Somehow, I had dipped into this place where I had completely "healed" and gotten over all the trauma and pain he caused, and I forgave it. I was ready to just have this super realistic relationship with him again. However, when he didn't answer the phone, it threw me into a pit of feeling pathetic and stupid, a feeling I knew too well.

I quickly ran out of cigarettes and reached out to many friends begging for them, and no one would bring them. *WOW, I REALLY AM alone.* I don't even have good friends that would bring me cigarettes when I'm stuck in Rehab. Now this is a new level of pathetic. Before long I was in a place where I really felt like this wasn't where I was supposed to be. I knew I should be somewhere because I still couldn't trust myself, but this wasn't it. It was keeping me alive but not helping me.

I had taken an LEC-5 test that scales the level of trauma you have experienced to determine the PTSD you have; they scale it on a range of 0-80. Taking this test, I was excited to share it with others to see how they scored (there was very little to do and be excited about here). The people I asked responded with 33, 27, 37, etc. I scored a **64**.

They gave the mandatory SI questionnaire every twenty-four hours to those who had expressed a desire to harm themselves. I took it so many times I memorized the questions and answered before prompted. It became so repetitive they finally let me have a one-on-one with the clinic director once a day instead, meeting with her instead of attending any family programs.

The reason for all that I am comes back to me. *What about all this trauma that could have brought me to the bottle?* No, I had a chemical imbalance in my brain that made me an alcoholic and this is all me.

I lived in a glorified adult summer camp of the worst design and the idea that I was defective was being shoved down my throat once every hour in "classes" I was being scheduled to attend. Don't get me wrong, drug and alcohol rehab is a much needed institution and does many wonderful things for people. However, how could I acknowledge mental health diagnoses with thousands of variants and still accept a program that was one-size-fits-all that told me I could come for thirty days and be healed? I think this was the point where I realized that I would never be healed.

I remember calling Desarae crying and telling her this wasn't it, but I didn't know what was. I threw myself into my relationship with God once again; I studied devotionals every night. I kept a journal which was just a journal of prayers asking God to fix me. No matter what I did, no matter what class I went to, none of this was new information to me; I was already practicing and trying most of it. *Where was the revelation I was looking for? The instant fix. Why wasn't being here fixing me?* AND I spent all fifteen minutes of phone time every day calling this man I had met in the mental hospital. Connecting with him like this was healthy and productive for what I was going through or so I thought.

In reality, I connected with another broken person who possibly was more fucked up than I was, so it made me feel better. Three weeks in, I was convinced that moving back to California was the best thing for me. I didn't want to go back to my job, and it scared me to go back to my life, so the right answer became running away yet again.

I spent the last remaining parts of my time at rehab just enjoying having "free food" and getting to know the girls better and trying to have fun. Every class I went to at that point, I just checked out mentally since I felt nothing was working. Half of this information didn't even apply to me and then if it did, I already knew or tried it before. I would lie down for most classes and fall asleep or daydream about how I envisioned my perfect life. My focus now was my plan once I got out and how fast I could move to California. I felt excited again; I could move back and no one I would meet as a new friend would know this was where I had been. I would be geographically closer to my children and hopefully be able to repair that relationship again. Again, I was avoiding it all.

Leaving rehab was a lot more overwhelming than I imagined. Try being away from your phone for thirty-two days and then getting it back and having 1000 missed text messages. One of those messages being from your father saying, "Do not contact me again, do not contact you sister or brothers either." This is a great start. *Was I surprised?* No.

Switching my focus, I needed to get rid of the stuff I didn't need to bring with me back to California as soon as possible. Purging materialistic items had always been a wonderful thing for me. I had sentiment to some things but not a lot. Part of me thought removing those items removed that memory or that segment of time and made me heal from it. Maybe it was because a part of me didn't think I deserved the nice things I had or things that made me happy. Maybe it was both.

Leaving Tennessee was shockingly easy, but then again, in my mind I felt like no one REALLY cared about me to begin with. I felt I had only formed surface friendships and all my core friends and family were out west and I never should have left to begin with. It was amazing what you can convince yourself of when you tried to justify running away, again.

The last stop before I left was a meeting with my Pastor. Since I met with him one-on-one the first time, he had experienced the loss of a child, so I truly felt like we could speak and connect on a level we hadn't before. I always felt like I connected with him. He was good at guiding me with the Lord and giving comfort and advice, but I felt now he would really have more understanding. Probably the best thing anyone has ever said to me through this entire journey was spoken in this meeting. He shared with me his own struggle in dealing with and healing from the loss of his son and soon after that, losing his father. Instead of approaching the situation of healing by "one more day without them," he approached it with "one day closer". In his case, one day closer to being with them in heaven and seeing them again.

In my case instead of being one more day without them, I was one day closer to seeing them again. Something so simple became so profound and changed my perspective and my pain; it impacted me stronger than any self-help book or any therapy session I had ever had. I always tried to be positive minded even when I sunk into this dark pit of depression, being positive and thinking of the same thing yet positively was something I had always strived for.

"One day closer."

So, I headed back to California, Palm Springs to be specific, to start my new life, be close to my family and friends and closer to my kids. I set my heart and mind that this was the first step to healing and moving forward and the first step to happiness. The drive

across country was an easy one; I imagined being able
to see everyone again regularly and being close to my
children in hopes of actually seeing them again one
day. The person I was going to live with was my favorite person on the planet, my "Brother". I was going to
have this exciting new beginning.

Or so I thought.

Moving there and seeing my family again was great;
the first few weeks were so ideal and perfect. I had
a fresh start with all the family I made myself, but I
struggled for weeks trying to find a job. I fell back into
drinking to numb the pain of moving and getting re-
acclimated to a new place and deal with the fact that I
couldn't get a good job. Desperately I wanted to have
and be fun again and I couldn't do it, but alcohol could.
It brought an overwhelming feeling that I was not good
enough and I sucked as a person, that's why I couldn't
find a reasonable job.

This decision to move back was supposed to answer
my prayers; it was to be the end-all-be-all to repairing
what was wrong. I fell, once again, into a tailspin of
believing the only answer was to kill myself. I knew
of a mountain pass nearby that took me to Idyllwild
where I could pull over into a lookout and see the entire valley. It was so pretty and peaceful at night and
I had planned to drive up there and kill myself with
pills and alcohol.

I felt like I had hit a wall of NO MATTER WHAT I DO,
NOTHING WORKED. I tried God; didn't work. I tried
rehab; didn't work. I tried coming back to where I was
from; didn't work. Nothing worked; I was out of options

and there was no other way to help me. I tried it all. I was helpless and useless, and my answer was to take my life.

Shortly after this episode, they offered me a job working in a chiropractic office, something I had done for years before doing hair. It paid very well, and I liked the people who worked there. This was one shining light for me to take me away from the act of suicide, to work my way out of this deep hole of depression I entered once again.

Then the pandemic hit.

At first it was very scary for me as it was for everyone, the unknown of what was happening and what was going to happen was very overwhelming and daunting. Initially, I was terrified and thought every single little sneeze or tickle of the throat I felt was Covid. That turned into a depressive thought of, even a pandemic where people were dying left and right isn't enough for my family to reach out and find me; they didn't even care if I'm dead or alive.

That was a heavy thought to bear, a weight that was drowning me. In the time everything had slowly shut down and it left nothing to do, my Brother made friends with some other tenants in the complex and constantly hung out with them or his new boyfriend. I was left alone. Initially, this added to my depression and feeling of worthlessness. I spent most of my time at work and then the rest of the time lying in my room watching TV and eating; I gained sixty pounds during this time.

As summer approached, I worked or was by the pool. My best friend in Tennessee was worried about me, being so reclusive was not good for anyone and we were all trying to figure out how to navigate this, worldwide. I didn't seem to care, and then I was upset about the fact that I was so alone; then I got really depressed about it. Little did I know the pandemic, and a lockdown was about to be the best thing that had ever happened to me, it allowed my perspective to change completely.

I could still work so I had purpose daily. My relationship with my closest friend at the time who was in Nashville had grown and blossomed into a friendship I had turned a blind eye to the whole time I lived there. A guard I had held up for so long came down and I could be completely vulnerable with her, confiding in her, and listening to her for the first time ever really, in such a raw way.

I spent my days, listening to devotionals, walking in the park, or lying by the pool which was my favorite thing to do. During these activities, I did them alone and processed and felt every single emotion necessary to work through and deal with all the emotional baggage and weights I struggled to carry around for the past eight years, if not longer. Never had I been in a situation in life where I was forced to sit with all my feelings and REALLY feel them. Not only that, but I was in an environment living with Brother where I felt completely secure and safe. Prior to this, I never felt like I was home anywhere. Also, there was always something else to do or some other way to distract myself.

A true pandemic lockdown forced me to face all my demons and really discover why, how, and what they were doing to me and how I could heal them. I could truly do the work and be honest with myself for the first time in my life; I wasn't clouding it with actions and activities to distract it all.

Let's break this down, shall we?

I am not a medical professional and am not a master of all things related to mental health. All I can do is share with you my experience and how I came to a better place of healing.

"To me you are displaying a lot of the symptoms and indications of borderline personality disorder."

So? I have multiple personalities? What is happening?
"What is that?"

"In fact, I would say you are also displaying the effects of C-PTSD along with the diagnosis you already have of GAD and Depression."

WOW. I am more fucked up than I thought.

Hearing these things for the first time living in a psych ward really didn't help normalize a mental health crisis. I am not saying it wasn't helpful or necessary, but it really put into perspective how bad my situation was.

The reason all this messed up stuff was happening and had happened in my life was because I was an alcoholic. What do these other things mean? I know I was depressed and had anxiety, but what did these other things mean? Instead of shoving them off and being afraid of them, I needed to educate myself.

I chased the dream of being fixed and healed and in mental health it just didn't exist. There wasn't an end to your treatment, there were only tools to help you deal, maintain, and LIVE WITH A DIAGNOSIS.

Once I sat down and truly researched my diagnosis and the symptoms and obstacles, I could face it became much easier. I wasn't obsessed with being perfect and healed; I was obsessed with doing my best every day. And if I had a bad day, I allowed myself to do so. This partnered with a correct and helpful medication regimen, I found myself in a healthy place I never dreamed I would arrive.

I knew at any point I could be back in that horrible place and that kept me healthy. Not being fooled because I had figured it all out and fixed it. Reading self-help books, going to AA meetings, being sober, throwing myself to God, are all wonderful tools that should be used as just that, tools. I clung to them like a magic potion that would erase all I had been through and continued to go through and with mental illness that was not a reality. Having mental illness does not mean you are broken or defective. To me, it should carry the same significance as having any other physical ailment: Diabetes, heart disease, cancer, etc. There was no shame with those illnesses and disorders, only a rallying of support and ways to LIVE WITH THE DIAGNOSIS. There was no reason the same can't be true for mental health.

This was the road I traveled realizing my mental health, what it meant, how I coped, and the things I realized I didn't even know were contributing to my demise.

DEPRESSION (major depressive disorder)

I think the first thing that comes to everyone's minds when they hear the word depression is the

PONY JEAN PARKER

stereotypical vision of someone curled up into a ball, can't leave their bed, crying for hours type of depression. I think that's what causes those of us that have depression into having trouble believing there is anything wrong that we need help with.

Depression can mean many things; it can mean being sad and crying for hours and it can mean faking a smile and feeling like you are slowly dying inside. I can't tell you how many times I moved on with my day and my life, but on the inside, I was so depressed and so down on myself that I never saw the light at the end of the tunnel. I imagined my life would always be depressive and, in fact, I thought it was what I deserved.

There have also been times, many times, I came face-to-face with a doctor telling him I had issues with anxiety, and he told me it was depression partnered with anxiety and I left the room frustrated and annoyed because I was adamant I was NOT depressed. I laughed and went out with my friends and (seemingly) enjoyed my life so, therefore, not depressed.

"For someone who is facing Major Depressive Disorder (MDD), internally they may feel lost, hopeless, helpless, guilty, angry, sad, anxious, or even suicidal. They may experience a lack of sleep, lack of pleasure, and decreased or increased appetite. Depression can feel debilitating. Someone may still feel isolated, even when surrounded by a sea of loving people." *Uncommon Signs and Symptoms Of Depression You Should Know About* (thepsychologygroup.com)

In doing research, I realized I displayed more uncommon signs of depression, such as:

Anger and Irritability: Have you ever had a day or a lot of days where even the sun shining outside is the most irritating thing that has ever happened to you? Nothing seems to go your way and the slightest thing sets you off in a rage and then you end up crying from frustration? Possibly coping or handling these emotions by sedating the feeling with drugs or alcohol? *Yeah, me neither (insert eye roll).*

Anxiety: Apparently, these two assholes go hand in hand. *Who knew?* I always viewed anxiety as its own thing, which it still is, but I did not know anxiety was a symptom of depression. The idea of even LIVING day-to-day sometimes became so overwhelming the only thing I could think to do was make myself sleep or I drank until I fell asleep. My mind went a million miles a minute with negative thoughts I couldn't control. Constant made-up scenarios of how I was a failure or how everyone hated me. It was never-ending and tiring and I felt it on a level I could never verbalize.

Overcompensation through perceived happiness: *STEP AWAY FROM THE FACEBOOK STATUS.* I can't tell you how many times in the past I lived there. Constantly posting what I was doing and how I was feeling, "I am having the best day ever!" "I can't believe how much progress I have made, and I am in such a better place now." "I have the best people in my life, and I am so blessed!" (This one is legitimately true, but why did I feel like I had to showboat it?)

One thing I learned on my journey and by seeing others and learning about theirs was if you are truly happy you don't feel the need to post incessantly about it, you are just happy living your life. I overcompensated for the chronic pain inside, and I didn't know what to do with it. Most commonly it was getting drunk and posting about how much fun I was having; in hindsight, I often wonder why someone didn't conduct an intervention sooner, but I was probably that convincing. I had an overwhelming fear of being a burden on people, so I guess I fooled everyone and was a very convincing actress.

There have been times I enjoyed being with friends and seemingly happy, but on the inside, I replayed my plan for suicide over and over to make sure I had it down how I wanted to commit it. Is there an academy award for pretending you're fine with your mental illness? I think I would win every year.

Weight gain/weight loss: For as long as I can remember, I was the same weight and height since I was thirteen. Tall and underweight. Depression makes your appetite go away OR makes you overeat. Why couldn't there be a sweet spot middle ground? Oh, that's right, it's depression. I have been constantly told my whole life, "You're too skinny. Eat a hamburger," "You don't look healthy," "Have you eaten enough today?" Fun fact: eating gave me anxiety. Also, when I'm depressed or in a very low mood, I have zero appetite. Even trying to force myself to eat makes me nauseous.

After I became sober, I gained a lot of weight and I thought, *wow, my age is finally catching up with me and I can't just eat whatever I want anymore.* NO. I had replaced alcohol with food and was eating all my emotions. I was depressed and eating to cope.

Insomnia or Lethargy: I remember when I came back from trying to see the kids for the first time. I didn't leave my bed for a week; I didn't even shower. I physically did not have the energy or power to even open my eyes. I often felt this after I had a bad day, or I was in a major depressive state. On the other hand, when I thought I was doing my best, I would sleep like six hours or fewer a night and thought it was because I was just doing really well.

Realizing depression is more than just a "state of mind" was hard. The physical effects it has on you are so overwhelming. I know for me I got to points where I physically felt ill or overly exhausted, then I got frustrated because I was so sick of feeling this way with major depressive disorder.

Uncontrollable emotions: I've heard the "joke" about "Which personality of hers will I get today?" or made the joke or retort that someone would never cheat on their partner because they had enough different personalities to make up different people all in one person. *Funny?* Yes, it can be. *Exhausting?* DEFINITELY.

I often found myself in moods where I was ticked off for no reason and there was nothing I could do to change it. Ten minutes later, I would cry uncontrollably, and then I felt guilty since it was very often disproportionate to the event that unfolded in front of me.

Loss of interest: I have so many things in life I find pleasure in doing, hobbies, and activities and such. I researched them on my phone and found a place and time to do them but ended up convincing myself that staying in bed was a much better option. I didn't have the desire to go out and enjoy things like I should, and to be completely honest, most of the time I had to force myself out. I daydreamed and obsessed about returning to my bed and couldn't even focus on what I was excited about going to do.

Self-Harm Behaviors: I remember the first time I self-harmed. The man I had a secret relationship with right after my first marriage was cheating on me and wanted to break up. I took a knife and cut down the outside of my forearms. Controlled pain in a moment of pain you can't control or get rid of is extremely satisfying. The idea that I have taken control over the pain I felt made me feel better.

Even as I write this, I understand how twisted it sounds, how jaded and clouded my thinking is about this. You shouldn't have to inflict physical pain on yourself to feel a release from internal pain or to feel better. This slowly escalated into using razor blades to cut my upper thighs because it was more hidden and only I saw it, and then I could pick at it incessantly and no one would see.

I also pick at my lips, the skin around my fingers, and the hair in my eyebrows to the point of creating sores and bleeding. I also pick at the skin inside of my nose because I have this subconscious idea that it makes me breathe better. I pick any scab I get on my body. It's like I have released some anxiety or poison by doing so. I have tried leaving my tweezers and other such tools in completely different rooms, but I will still get up every five or six minutes and pick at something again before returning to bed, up and down and up and down over and over every night for a couple hours until I finally realize what is happening and tell myself, "OK you are not allowed to get up anymore."

"Depression is not an emotion; it's a mental illness. If you know someone struggling with a mental illness, do not judge them. Provide support and lovingly encourage them to get help from a professional. If you identify with the symptoms above, know that hope and change are possible. You are not alone. Invest in yourself by reserving time with a therapist because you are worth it." *Uncommon Signs and Symptoms Of Depression You Should Know About* (thepsychologygroup.com)

ANXIETY (generalized anxiety disorder or GAD)

There's anxiety and then there's GAD. I think we all, at some point in our lives or days and weeks, deal with anxiety before a big work meeting, public speaking, etc. The difference between anxiety and GAD is the following.

Anxiety not related to a mood disorder relates to a specific situation or problem and lasts only as long as that situation or problem and is proportional to the situation or problem and is a realistic response to the problem. Situations related to the ones I described above.

For the longest time, I ignored the feelings of anxiety I had because I assumed it was normal and everyone felt the same things. I just felt like, "Man, this being alive shit sucks. I can never relax."

An example of things I do would be, carrying every scenario in a situation all the way out and imagine all possible negative conclusions to where I subconsciously create them to happen to satisfy my anxiety and validate it.

Difficulty concentrating and feeling like my mind goes blank. Have you ever stared at a written word and reread it for ten minutes straight or hit rewind on a TV show or movie you were watching multiple times because you have taken in the information auditorily, yet you have ABSOLUTELY NO IDEA WHAT YOU JUST READ OR HEARD? *Yeah, me neither.*

Difficulty with handling uncertainty or indecisiveness. I often boasted about my ability to be organized and how much I loved it, when deep down inside, my entire day had to be organized and planned out or I lost my shit. The thought of being impulsive (unless in a BPD rage) terrifies me. I was constantly going over in my mind repeatedly what I was about to do, what time I'd do it, when I'd be done, what the place looked like, how long it took to get there, etc. and then when that was over, I'd start from the beginning and do it all over again.

The inability to relax, the restlessness, the inability to set aside or let go of a worry, persistent obsession with concerns large or small that's out of proportion to impact an event. Round it all up by worrying about excessively worrying are also part of this diagnosis.

The self-harm of skin picking also comes into play here, more specifically with the lips, nails and eyebrows. Especially the lips and zoning out in disassociation while doing so and just replaying imaginary chaotic "could be" events over and over in my head.

From a very young age, I remember taking up the habit of looking at written words, most of the time on signs, like street signs or billboards and counting out the letters in my head repeatedly figuring out how they count out in a numerical succession (even amounts, by threes, etc.) When that wasn't sufficient, it escalated to counting them out in my mind, and also with successive breathing. Breathing in and out with each letter of the phrase. Then it became counting off in my head, with breathing and counting with my actual fingers. I would do this for twenty or thirty minutes at a time, focusing on the same words or phrase.

The physical symptoms, I think are the most frustrating. I have learned positive coping skills over the years that I have used to distract myself mentally or change my way of thinking to break myself out of an anxious mental moment, but the physical ones, there was nothing I could do.

Being easily startled, the fatigue, headaches, irritability, body pains, sweating, trembling, and my absolute favorites: nausea, diarrhea, irritable bowel syndrome.

I think the GI and IBS symptoms are the earliest symptom I can remember. I lived in a constant state of anxiety as a young teenager, directly following the incident with my older brother, and around the same time, I started realizing I was being raised in a cult and it was bullshit. Yet, I felt like I had no other choice but go along and be a part of it. I was constantly in the bathroom with indigestion and diarrhea. I chalked it all up to having a sensitive stomach and maybe needing to eat a bland diet. It was so bad my parents finally took me to the doctor. They did all kinds of blood tests and fecal tests (fun shit), and everything came back normal. I remember the end result; they told my dad that it was because of anxiety and stress. His response was to laugh and make the comment, "Stress?!?! What stress does she have in her life? If it's stress, then I should live on the toilet." This symptom I was living with was easily gone and forgotten by my parents as being an issue.

I often feel as if I am sick, my body hurts in specific places, the fatigue as if I have the flu and have no energy, trembling from nausea. GAD is easily one of my most harsh and stressful diagnoses. Living in a constant and I mean CONSTANT state of heightened awareness of your heart racing and the fight-or-flight feeling you get like when someone scares you, the inability to relax or shut your mind off, incessantly analyzing every interaction you have at any point of any day, causes the most tiresome feeling I could ever describe to you.

Yes, we all have bad days where we second guess and worry but imagine doing it from the second you wake up to the moment you fall asleep and then manifest it in your dreams. I worry if I got enough sleep. I panic, thinking I don't have enough time to get ready that morning and then rush through it at top speed because I have an anxiety attack that I won't make it on time. I over analyze every single interaction with anyone, especially at work, and immediately internalize any off tone or quick retort or passive interaction, feeling as if I have messed up in some major way and EVERYONE

HATES ME. I am worthless, I suck, and I can't come back from it.

That turns into me obsessing over what things need to be done when I get home from work and then not doing any of them. Lying in bed watching some TV show but not actually internalizing any of the dialogue because I am replaying the day in my head and over analyzing how I could have done EVERYTHING differently before I fall asleep creating made up scenarios in my head and replaying them all to the worst possible outcome or conclusion.

There is not one point in this description that I embellished or exaggerated. In fact, you should probably take all of this and intensify this 15x or more and then you can meet me on my daily level.

Complex PTSD (C-PTSD)

Although not favorably diagnosed by most, the true difference between PTSD and complex PTSD is the times the traumatic event has happened. Being robbed at gunpoint or being in a terrible car accident are examples of PTSD. Enduring a repeated child abuse or being in a physically violent relationship are examples of Complex PTSD.

With PTSD, you often experience the trauma reliving through nightmares or flashbacks, situations that remind you of the trauma and affect your "triggers", hyperarousal continuously being in the state of a high alert, constantly believing you are not safe, and you are not safe from those around you in your life and the "wonderful" negative self-view you have of yourself.

I constantly have nightmares that relive each of my traumas over and over to the point of reality that when I wake up, I cannot figure out if it has actually happened or not. I am in a state of haze or a place between sleeping and awake, immediately feeling the physical effects of this; heart racing, sweating, shaking, or trembling, and there is nothing I can do to change that. The physical effects take over outside of my control. No matter how much I do to help myself, there are no proven treatments or medications to remove this from happening completely. Having that reality is exhausting, realizing I will forever have to deal with a PTSD nightmare is enough to understand why people reach the point of wanting to end their own lives.

For the longest time, I dealt with triggers within society that I didn't initially realize that's what was happening. I watched the movie *Gladiator* with Russell Crowe for the first time, and it caused an extreme amount of nausea and trembling when it became apparent two of the characters were involved in an incestuous relationship. Any type of behavior that involved a narcissistic being or cult-like behavior and my fight-or-flight kicked in and I became confused and disoriented and ill. Living with symptoms like these will NEVER go away. I will get to a place where I can better handle them, but they will never STOP. That to me, is the most daunting and horrible feeling I can imagine.

Feeling like I am not good enough for someone and they choose to leave me, whether it be romantic or platonic relationship, is a huge trigger for me. I immediately panic and forget everything I feel and do whatever I can to ensure they will not leave me. If they continue to do so anyway, then I relive my family disowning me all over again as if it had just happened. That is another thing that happened when my kids refused to see me after I tried to go see them. I relived losing them all over again from the beginning. I was right back on that bathroom floor in my Las Vegas house, crying and immobile, laid out on the tile floor, wanting to die.

Distrusting and Isolating from others: For the longest time I just thought everyone sucked, I constantly second guessed everyone's intentions and assumed they were lying or pretending to like me. Finding the smallest thing to have a problem with and being upset and figuring I just didn't need them in my life, while in reality I was leaving them before I could be left. Granted, I think there was some sort of level of people "not getting it" or not understanding me, but not to the extent that I kicked people out of my life constantly.

I would fall into episodes of isolation and make myself be alone by telling myself I was truly alone and not telling anyone how I was feeling or just pretending I was OK. It did nothing but further serve the depression of a false narrative I had written about being alone. I think losing my family and my entire social structure had left me with feeling this was what I deserved, to be alone and that's why I caused that for myself. My family didn't even want me or care, so there was no possible way anyone could feel like that for me.

I remember one time I took a road trip with a friend to her hometown; we went in her car. As soon as I got there, I started panicking because all I could think was, *these people are not Jehovah's Witnesses, therefore they are dangerous, as they have always taught me. Here I was at her boyfriend's house STUCK with people I don't trust. Who were these people, really? Was I in danger?* I was pretty sure I was in danger. These were the PTSD thoughts going through my head after being raised and indoctrinated into this cult.

Getting Startled Easily: For as long as I remember, at a good horror movie is exactly where I wanted to be. I never get scared easily, only in those moments where something pops out at you intentionally for the jump factor. Ever since everything happened, I startle very easily: a loud noise, a sudden movement, someone walking around a corner at the same time I am. And it's not just, "Oh you scared me," like a little jump; it's like a full-blown panic attack, adrenaline running through my body and my heart pounding, taking minutes for me to calm down. Along with it comes the feeling like I'm in trouble or something bad is happening. It's awful and what's even more awful is not being able to control the physical feeling of it once I realize nothing is wrong. It's like my body takes over and has a mind of its own.

Hypervigilance: Merriam Webster defines extreme or excessive vigilance (hypervigilance) as the state of being highly or abnormally alert to potential danger or threat. Now, I understand through common sense and staying aware of your surroundings that we are all alert to potential danger or threat. Hypervigilance, though, is the state of constant high alert to danger. So, the panic feeling you get when you think you're in trouble or you're scared, it's that except literally all the time. No matter what you do, you mentally and physically feel that all day.

For the longest time, because I had chosen not to speak up and speak out about how I felt inside, I weirdly assumed that everyone had a heightened state of hypervigilance and anxiety. It made me never truly be able to rest.

I am constantly tense and on edge. My jaw hurts all the time from clenching it nonstop all day. My shoulders are hard as boulders from being tense. It literally causes physical I have pain in every limb every day because I am that tense EVERYWHERE and hold my muscles so tightly it causes fatigue. When I sleep, you would think it would get better. It doesn't. I wake up feeling sore and physically tired, day after day after day. It truly gets to where I am s physically and mentally exhausted, all I can do is cry.

Along with all of that, I am constantly in a state of high alert; I always sit in a room with my back to a wall so no one and nothing can be behind me, constantly scanning the room, watching, and observing everyone's behavior. (Fun fact that comes along with that is I am paranoid thinking all eyes are on me, and everyone is staring at me, judging me like they can read my mind).

Hypersensitivity: My hypersensitivity comes into play with sensory actions. Loud noises, particularly like a crowded restaurant, a concert, really just going anywhere that provides a lot of stimulation and I immediately have a fight-or-flight response and I want to leave immediately. It's frustrating for me because I was never like this before. I could go anywhere with a lot of people, and I was fine (granted, I was highly intoxicated usually as well). Now, after all this time and effects of trauma, I feel like I can't function as a "normal person" with sensory issues. I panic in a grocery store or Target. *How much does that suck?*

Dissociation: "Dissociation is a break in how your mind handles information. You may feel disconnected from your thoughts, feelings, memories, and surroundings. It can affect your sense of identity and your perception of time." *Dissociation: Causes, Diagnosis, Symptoms, and Treatment* (webmd.com)

Dissociating is one of the hardest things to convey and have others understand if they don't go through it themselves. It can happen for moments or days. For me, it's daily, often for twenty to thirty minutes and sometimes for hours.

I think the easiest way to explain it is like a really depressing out-of-body experience. You completely disconnect from society, your surroundings, and even yourself. I will literally sit wherever I am and wonder how I'm a human being, how is the world even a world. Logic and concern all leave the building and I feel like a body having no attachment. I cannot comprehend simple conversation or interactions and often "stare off into space". On top of that, it is physically exhausting, like taking a sedative. For me, it commonly comes after a time of extreme anxiety, overwhelming experience, or heightened panic. I can't logically comprehend that I have to be a human being.

Borderline Personality Disorder or BPD (also known as emotional dysregulation disorder; a mental disorder characterized by unstable moods, behaviors, and relationships)

As far back as I can remember, I always thought I had a bad or short temper. My father displayed the same type of reactions, so I assumed I had the same. (His truly was just a temper issue.) *Was I sensitive?* There was no way. *Over reactive?* Definitely. *Constantly grasping at getting people to understand me and see how I was feeling was normal or correct?* CONSTANTLY.

An intense fear of abandonment: Since an early age and growing up JW, I have always felt this way, always feeling I was not good enough or something was wrong with me, so I had an innate fear of abandonment. It carried over into every single relationship I have ever had, whether friend or romantic. One slight misstep and I thought I was going to lose this person; I was going to show how inadequate and worthless I was and worthy of abandonment. This has always caused severe people pleasing and the endless desire to "save" people.

Another harmful defense mechanism is to avoid reality at all costs. In my mind, this was all real. Often to where I would end the connection to be in charge of the abandonment. I was going to leave or create a narrative, causing the other person to get rid of me to feed the idea I had that I was unworthy and prone to abandonment.

I wish I could explain how deep-rooted this is, convey to you to understand how absolutely gut-wrenching and real this feels. I feel it like a physical pain. My soul actually aches, and tears build up in the back of my throat when I focus on it.

A pattern of unstable intense relationships: Coming from someone who has been married twice and engaged once without marriage (I will not talk about that one). I can definitely tell you this is real.

When I connect with someone on a romantic level, it must be fast, hard, and intense. I want to be with them forever within the first few weeks and want the feeling reciprocated immediately. Fast, hard, and intense or it's not real. I become severely codependent and unrealistically attached to the point of ignoring my own wants and needs and adopting all of theirs for fear if I wanted something for myself, they would leave.

Looking back on all the men I have been in "serious" relationships with, they have always been narcissistic and sexually demanding. In the beginning, I thought I had a healthy view of sexuality and then quickly it turned into they only wanted me for sex, and I became very physically withdrawn and uninterested. As fast as it started, it quickly turned to self-sabotage as the fear of abandonment came in and ruined it to make them leave before I could be left. A never-ending cycle of this for the last twenty-two years or so. *How exhausting!*

Rapid changes in self-identity and self-image: If I had a dollar for every time I had a new idea, goal, or focus in life, I would be a millionaire. I can never settle for just being stagnant and content. I constantly have new obsessions of ideals I must research and plan on executing until the next one comes along; I am never satisfied. This includes myself, my appearance, my values, my opinions, all of it. My hair, my clothes, my accessories, everything is constantly changing. I am never content with myself.

Periods of stress related paranoia and loss of contact with reality: I live in a state of stress with no end in sight. My life and its events are 200% worse than anything anyone has ever been through. I have periods where it all is too much to handle and causes me physical pain and then I zone out and have majorly depressive and dangerous intrusive thoughts like killing myself, driving my car into a wall on the freeway, jumping off a tall bridge. Everyone would be so much better off without me. I daydream about the people who may or may not show up to my funeral, who may or may not think about me every year on the anniversary of my death, or who will casually forget about me three years after I have gone.

Impulsive or risky behavior: I feel like most of my life as an adult definitely portrayed this behavior–a lot of sexual promiscuity, heavy drinking which led to impulsive, dangerous decisions. I think I have had upwards of thirty+ jobs in my life. As soon as one thing goes wrong, I'm convinced I have to leave and find another job. In the moment, I convince myself that this is me "letting go" and just getting out of my mind and being free, but it's another side effect of my illness and losing control completely and dangerously. The impulsive behavior makes me feel free and "normal", I instantly feel grounded and like I have a good hold on my life. The rush is short-lived until the next impulsive decision. It's scary how much a damaged brain can convince you your actions are normal and make sense.

Suicidal threats or behavior or self-injury: With BPD, I feel like it is all or nothing, the slightest inconvenience, and the only answer is to die. The intrusive thoughts are real and intense. I got cut off on the way to work and my first client acted like they didn't like the job I did on their hair, so I should just go kill myself. It sounds dramatic, I get that, but I cannot explain how realistic and accepting this is in my mind. Self-injury being the answer when the pain in your mind is so intense you turn to self-injury because now you have control over the physical pain. Sounds strange but, it works.

Wide mood swings lasting from hours to days/Ongoing feelings of emptiness/Inappropriate feelings of anger: I feel like this goes along well with one of the ways they recognize BPD (Emotional Dysregulation Disorder) often confused with Bipolar Disorder. I have touched on this along the way with describing how the other symptoms are portrayed and/or affect me. Emotions affect me so deeply that I wish they did not. I wish there were a valid reason behind it all, but sometimes there isn't.

Sometimes I have an overwhelming feeling of shame or as if I am in trouble and there is no rhyme or reason behind it, which makes the feeling that much more shaming and intense. Sometimes I wake up that way with no reason and sometimes it is in response to doing something I enjoy and having fun. A lot of times lately, it happens in response to eating a good meal; like I enjoy something so much my body defaults to shame or anger in response because the good feeling should not be happening. The slightest inconvenience can make me mad as well and my internal thoughts are like, *Seriously, why are you THIS MAD?* and I have no clue why it's happening. I cannot shut it off.

Estrangement

Being estranged by a family member or, in my case members, is one of the most painful feelings I have ever experienced. The unexpectedness, ambiguous nature, the powerlessness intensified it. It creates the social disapproval. I was already living a life as an outcast and feeling like my being was a disapproval and defective. To sit in the courtroom and have my whole life pulled out from under me and lose everyone on the same day at the same time in a matter of minutes, I can never explain this feeling to another person.

We are biologically attached to others, especially family, and when this structure is ripped from us, it throws us into an unknown societal change as well that is so hard to process and accept. The lost family is physically absent, yet the memories are present, causing a feeling similar to that of grieving the death of a loved one. But in the back of your mind, you know they are still alive and just don't want you. It also, creates a loss of closure and not knowing if they will ever return; leaving you often wondering and ruminating about the event and about your relationship.

Many people develop such embarrassment and shame they go to great lengths to hide the situation from being found out. We are born with an innate need for family and a community sandbox and when that goes missing, it is severely detrimental as a human being. I am constantly triggered on Mother's Day or my children's birthdays, or when I knew my family would get together and I knew I was missing out on it. As mad as I am at my family for creating this estrangement, I still longed for the connection and familiarity I once had with them. Although my upbringing was not ideal and filled with mind-altering trauma, it wasn't all bad. There are parts I wish I could go back and experience once again and be a part of, and I know I never will.

Religious Trauma Syndrome

Although highly controversial as at the time of publishing, this condition is still not recognized in the DSM or DSM-5 [*The Diagnostic and Statistical Manual of Mental Disorders* (DSM) is the handbook used by health care professionals in the United States and much of the world as the authoritative guide to the diagnosis of mental disorders]. This is a condition experienced by those leaving a high control religion (or cult) and coping with the damage of the indoctrination. The symptoms are cognitive, emotional, social, and cultural. Things such as:

- Negative feelings about self-ability and self-worth
- Depression, anxiety, and grief
- loss of social network and social awkwardness
- difficulty belonging and feeling like a "fish out of water"

Causes can come from things such as: Suppression of normal child development, damage to normal thinking abilities such information being limited/controlled and patriarchal power.

RTS causes struggling with black and white thinking, irrational thinking, difficulty trusting oneself, low self-esteem, feeling indebted to a group of people, skewed views on sex and sexual nature, discipline, emotional regulations, relationships, and self-expression. From an early age (or whatever age you come into contact with it), you are shamed and guilted into conforming to a mental test of believing in an unknown and unprovable source or "salvation" and the slightest misstep or challenge of said beliefs lands you as an outcast and a horrible human being.

Growing up, I knew no differently from the stories and beliefs fed to me as a child. It was the only way of life and the only way of being. There was no question. In fact, as a grade school child, I felt bad for those who didn't believe as the Org taught me because they were going to die in Armageddon, and they were horrible for not believing what I did. I was guilted and shamed constantly into believing and acting perfectly or God hated me and so did my family and friends and I was going to die. I don't think there needs to be any further explanation for a so-called religion to teach you that if you do not say and do exactly as they demand, you would die.

Think about that for a second, you are teaching a five-year-old if they don't act within the lines of some rules a man made up claiming to have heard it from God, you're going to die, and everyone hates you. *How is this not child abuse or not recognized by more people the type of mental abuse and trauma this is for people?*

Becoming mentally and physically rid of these teachings at thirty has only given me ten years to reverse the damage that has been done. Did you know sometimes when I go out with my friends and enjoy myself that the next day, I can't leave my bed because of the overwhelming guilt and shame I have from enjoying myself? That I still lay in bed at night terrified that the end of the world is coming while I sleep, and I will be killed? That I am deserving of every horrible and unjust thing that has ever happened to me because I am an unbeliever who turned against God and deserve these injustices? I deserved my children taken from me because I am a horrible human being.

The thoughts that weigh heavy on my mind could never be articulated clearly enough for you to even experience a glimpse of the constant mental anguish this has caused me and will forever cause me.

The clarity that came along with this made me realize that coming back to California was not the answer. I did not move back in healing; I ran away in terror of facing all my demons and truly doing the work to heal myself. I had given up and ran as if a change of scenery was a magical antidote for my pain. I was trying to go back to a life and a person who was no longer there, no longer living. I realized I was now in limbo between making true strides in this moment to heal and moving forward or going backwards and living in this pain for the rest of my life; a life that probably would have been cut short quickly. I was determined to move forward.

"One step closer"

Along with that, sure I had the love and support of my family back on the west coast, but what I soon realized was what an incredible and large support system I truly had in Nashville that I turned away from and ignored because I felt like I didn't deserve it. I felt so alienated and alone because I put myself there and refused all the support from many people who loved me and wanted to be there for me. I had made a mistake.

Moving to California was not what would fix me, sitting with my feelings and truly processing them and forcing myself to be uncomfortable was what would fix me. Realizing that accepting a diagnosis or accepting a trait about myself wasn't how I would be fixed. I had spent the last three years running around accepting I was broken, and I had anxiety and depression, and then C-PTSD, and Borderline Personality Disorder.

Before my diagnoses, it was just, "I'm an alcoholic and that's my excuse." What I had actually done was search for whatever the "answer" was for why I was broken. In my mind, accepting that answer meant I was fixed and solved. Everything was fine now and when those things obviously didn't happen, it enraged my struggling. What I needed to realize and accept was that I would never have a cure for my trauma, for my diagnoses, for any of my pain. What I needed to realize was that I had these amazing tools at my fingertips to help me LIVE with them. I had developed poor coping skills by using alcohol, men, and self-harm to cope when the work that was needed was within. I formed this idea, as I'm sure many of us have, that I had to fix everything and be over all of it. When in reality, the best I was going to achieve is how to live with my diagnoses and live a beautiful life.

Once I had realized and accepted that, everything became so much easier. I realized how far I had come and how much I had actually done and put effort into healing. I had been there all along.

During my time back in California, I drove to the house I was raised in on McLaughlin Avenue. Every once in a while, during these eight years I would pull up the image of this house on the internet just to see their cars, see if they still lived there, in the home that, at times, was filled with laughter and wonderful memories. About a year prior, I pulled it up and the front yard displayed a for sale sign. I found the listing and scrolled through pictures of my childhood home, empty. Visually scanning each picture, recalling the specific memories I made in each of these now empty rooms.

So, I drove there, walked up and knocked on the door. There was a family who lived there now. A husband, wife, and their infant daughter. A stark emotion of curiosity as the wife opened the door after I knocked.

"Hi there! I know this is odd, but I used to live in this house, and I just kind of wanted to come and see it."

Before I could continue, an extreme excitement escaped her lips, "Oh my goodness! We have heard all about your family and have always wondered who you were! Please come in! I would love for you to see it and tell me about the house."

Crossing that threshold was like going back in time. Although the colors of the walls had changed and the carpet was now removed, exposing the original wood floors from 1940, it was all the same.

We went from room to room; I told her the stories of my family. The happy memories and whose room was whose. They completely remodeled the bathroom and the kitchen, but all the touches that made it recognizable were still there. Times we played games in the dining room, the nights spent in the living room laughing with friends from the congregation, the time my daughter was running through the kitchen and split her eyebrow hitting the countertop, the backyard where we used to play as children, my bedroom where I would do schoolwork and watch football every Sunday, my mother's craft room where we would watch fashion designer shows and critique gowns celebrities wore at award shows.

It also encased the bad: the time my brother tried to force me to have sex with him, the time my father kicked me out of the house when I was pregnant, the time I realized and pointed out to my mother that all the years in this house there was not one picture of me hung on any of the walls and none of us had ever noticed for over ten years at that point. The times I laid in bed upset; I wasn't good enough for God. The times I cried in the shower so no one would know.

As scary as the idea of this was, and even though it invoked feelings and memories of both the good and the bad, it gave me allowance to look back on all of it and be OK. The bad times and moments spent in pain were just that, but I didn't have to use those to define my past life in entirety.

Not all the times were bad. I had many beautiful memories that were OK to look back on in fondness and with love and appreciation and happiness. Living in these memories and enjoying the emotions of happy that came along with them didn't mean I was in denial of the pain I suffered there, and I didn't have to feel guilty or shameful for loving them. My life was not entirely awful. Yes, the core things indoctrinated into me shaped me horribly and caused such tumultuous aftershocks that I carry to this day but, it's OK to be happy too. Even if they were no longer in my life, I can enjoy the happy things in my memories without feeling like I was doing my mind a disservice.

I knew what I needed to do.

What was really going to "fix" me was using these tools and giving myself grace to be broken and putting my best foot forward every day.

There would never be a day when my diagnoses are healed and that's OK. I spent so many years fighting for the solution I would never find, and you know what, THAT'S OK. My life can still be beautiful. I can still be a worthy human being deserving of all the beautiful things that come along with the love and support of your loved ones.

Nashville was my home now, and I needed to return there and to myself. Once I let everyone know of my decision to return, I was met with overwhelming support of my decision. They could see the difference in me and knew this time I was going there because I WANTED TO and not because I was running away from something. Nashville was my true home, and they could see why.

These years I was always addressed as Pony. I rarely even told people my birth name unless it was on a form at a doctor's office or something. Honestly, some friendships I made over these years, they don't even know what my legal name was. The moment I arrived as the completion to the person I was and the person I became led me to finally put into motion my legal name change, ridding myself of the birth name they gave me that associated me with a family I would never relate to again. I needed to be 100% completely ME now.

I needed a last name, though.

I remember the moment I was sitting in my room and was like, *huh; I need a different last name, but what should it be?* In a flash, I replayed all the moments with Desarae and her family, the moments that truly taught me what being a family really meant and how to love. The things she showed and taught me led me to cultivate genuine relationships with others that were healthy and unconditional.

There is no other last name I could think of that would be better.

Pony Jean Parker

Jean was my grandmother's middle name and the one part of my family I never wanted to let go of. Her memory and legacy still live very deeply in my heart, and I know she is watching me from wherever she is and is so proud of me.

I let Desarae know of my wish and she became immediately emotional. Her family was so incredibly proud and grateful and happy I chose to be a part of their family in this way.

"We are so proud of you and so happy to have you be a part of this family."

A sentence I had been spending the last eight years of my life searching for in all the people I met. The toxic friends I tried to save. The relationships with narcissistic men who used me for sex, and the relationships with women who abused me mentally. All the bottles of alcohol I drank. All the things I threw myself into avoiding my haunted realities. I had been exhausting myself for years searching for this in others and things to replace the wounds of my family, and I had it all along in not only her family but all my other close friends. I just needed to ALLOW IT.

On August 12, 2020, I legally became Pony Jean Parker. To finally be recognized as my true self, an overwhelming amount of peace washed over me. It removed the bonds of my past, and the part of me that still held me to the standards and ideals of those who ruined me years before. It allowed me to have grace and understanding for myself in knowing that the work I had done for myself this time was real and healthy. My road will never be easy, but it was mine. I could have bad days and bad moments, but that didn't define me as a person and that it was OK. Emotions I felt were valid and real. Emotions were neither good nor bad, they just were.

For once I was not imprisoned by my trauma but accepted and forgiven. The only thing that can HELP was me, not a church, not alcohol, not endlessly trying to help others. Only the understanding and patience I gave myself helped me day to day. That's all I needed. That brought me this peace.

November 7, 2020
Hey if you wanna talk let me know.
Dad

I was getting ready to go to my favorite coffee shop to continue writing my story. I came out of the shower to see what time it was and had a text on my phone from a 310 number I didn't have saved as a contact. For a split second I thought, *well that's weird.* I finished reading the phone number and realized it was my dad's cell phone number. I panicked for a moment and rushed to unlock my phone to read it: *Hey if you wanna talk let me know. Dad.*

I stared at my phone for a minute–it's almost like a ghost from the past presenting itself just in time to mess up your day. Initially, I was surprisingly calm; I think it was a moment of shock. Immediately I called one of my best friends, "I just got out of the shower and found that my dad texted me."

"How do you feel about that?" they asked.

My gut reaction was as if I reached out to him and expected he was just going to tell me how I fucked everything up, fucked my kids up, and would really give it to me. It's sad to say that would be my gut reaction to seeing a text from my father, but it's not without basis. My father had always been a very intimidating man who thought, as the father of our family, he was and always would be in charge of everyone and made all the decisions. His judgement, as well as the PTSD from growing up in a high control religion, made me feel like no matter what I did, I was a failure; I was a shameful person, an awful human being. I automatically default-ed to these ways of thinking.

Then I thought, well if he wanted to be negative, he would continue to ignore my existence and pretend he's down a daughter/child. That quickly led into bouts of crying and anger thinking, *I literally called you eleven months ago, and you told me never to contact you again and now you want to talk to me? Like, can I talk to YOU? You threw me away like TRASH. You literally were the front-runner reason for me losing my children. Having them taken from me because you believed the lies of their father instead of trusting your own daughter. How dare you! Who are you to want to talk?*

My dad literally broke my heart. I would never wish on my worst enemy the ways I felt over the past eight years. The level of mind games it did to me when I was disowned by my own parents for believing and think-ing differently, humiliated in front of a court about it, hearing the lawyers read off all the most horrible things my family thought I was, and sitting blind-sided, left to feel like a complete waste of a person.

I kept thinking, *Do you know I thought about you before I tried to commit suicide and all the times I con-templated doing so? I sat there and daydreamed that you didn't care if I killed myself because you hated me any-way? At what point did you stop and realize the trauma and shame and pain and guilt you caused your own child that led them to imagine such horrible things? Are you try-ing to clear your own conscience? Is your health declining and you were trying to "make amends" before you passed? Was this a completely selfish move on your part to release your guilt for no other reason than to make yourself feel better? Or was this genuine and you realized you made a horrible mistake and wanted to apologize to me? Tell me you have missed me, and you realized you broke my heart and tore my children from me. Which is it? Do I want to take that risk? Do I want to find out which way this was going to fall?*

I spent so many nights crying, wishing I could call you and tell you what I'm doing with my life, so you could know how proud of me you could be; for you to tell me you love me, that I am your daughter, and you supported me. I sobbed uncontrollably, wishing I could just hear your voice. You did this to me. YOU DID THIS TO ME. Can I forgive this?

Thoughts continued to race and a part of me thought, *this is my chance to show them not being a Jehovah's Witness anymore didn't ruin my life.* Sure, they ruined my life by facilitating having my children taken from me, making me feel like I was a waste of a human being, and creating PTSD for me. But my life, for the most part since leaving, had grown in some very beautiful ways. I have friends I consider family who love me unconditionally. I grew in my trade. I moved across the country. I learned I shouldn't be ashamed or hide who I am, that there is nothing wrong with who I am. Then I thought, *I don't have to prove ANYTHING to them.* I need nothing to be validated nor feel like something had to be justified in their eyes and accept me.

I went on thinking this was my opportunity to put on the heart and mind of Christ and show them what a true Christian is; show them outside of that cult is where God really is. Jesus said in the Bible regarding how many times we are to show forgiveness, "I do not say to you seven times, but seventy times seven." I struggled to figure out how to embody Christ and also heal my anger and protect myself from being hurt again. This wasn't the first time, although the most damaging time, they'd hurt me. *So, how did I keep from getting hurt again?* I was not sure that I could survive another annihilation by their hands.

Why couldn't I sit next to someone, anyone who had all the answers to everything in life and look them in their eyes and ask them what I should do? Why wasn't there some sort of magical answer to all of this?

The answer came in time, in just a few days. In moments like this and some in the past, my initial course of action was to react quickly and fueled by emotion. Instead, I meditated on all of it, and it became such a healing moment. A moment of focus and clarity. I reminisced about all the good times, and all the bad. I thought about all the nights I laid in bed crying for my family, the many moments I experienced over these last eight years that my initial gut reaction was to call them and share those moments with them.

And then I thought of my son. When we first reconnected verbally, one of the first things he expressed to me was he forgave me, without question. He said he didn't know whose fault it was, and it didn't matter. I was his mother, and I would be a part of his life. My then seventeen-year-old son could put on the maturity of a wise adult and express this to me and mean it. *How could I not do the same? How could I not try at least have one conversation and see how I felt?*

Days after his text, I texted my dad back and said I would like to have a conversation with him. We made plans for the following night to speak.

When my phone rang and I answered and I first heard his voice, it was like no time had passed. I think there was an obvious level of nervousness between us both. He sounded the same. He spoke to me calmly and almost endearingly. We made awkward small talk. "Where do you live? How do you like it there? What kind of car do you drive now?" I explained I was doing well. I had a beautiful life in Nashville that I loved and a career I adored. He told me my mother and he were doing well; they liked their new house. I told him I went to our family home after they moved out and the new tenants let me in. It was a sweet moment with them.

We only spoke for about twenty minutes about nothing, small talk catching up with a familiar stranger. He told me he hired a private investigator to find me, that when Covid happened he wanted to make sure I was OK. Hearing that made me so confused and also, why did it take him this long?

The end of the call came quickly after this admission and he asked if it would be OK to call me again sometime, to check in on me and make sure I was OK. Although I hesitated initially out of protection and confusion from the things he had just told me, I let him know that would be fine and then he followed it up with the comment, "You know, it's very important to me to make sure you're OK."

I felt like someone had hit me in the chest. It took my breath out of my body; it had knocked the wind out of me. I have never been shot, but in this moment, I imagined this was what it felt like, a searing indescribable pain I couldn't describe accurately no matter how hard I could try. I quickly ended the phone call.

It is? It's important to you?

Eight years later, we were standing in this statement. That's what we were doing. I cried so hard; I cried all the tears I held in times I didn't allow myself to cry. Tears so hot they felt as if they were burning my cheeks, fighting to catch my breath. Maybe it was this, maybe it was all of it. For eight years, I imagined this moment. I imagined running to his arms and being embraced and hearing, "I am so sorry for leaving you". I had imagined a complete moment of never acknowledging my presence ever again, and somehow here we were in the middle.

Although it felt as if no time had passed, a lot of the conversation felt very foreign. Like we were talking about a ghost or someone who had died. Small references made to the family, the past, and my birth name; I felt like a stranger. I was no longer that person. I had grown and evolved and healed in so many ways and was a completely different person.

I stood in this moment of choosing between either I could let this ruin me or I could take the moment for what it was and move on. I dreamed about this moment, but it didn't happen how I would have ultimately desired. It could be a catalyst to spiral again and deep dive into a world of pain and self-harm, toxic behaviors, and unhealthy coping mechanisms and I didn't think anyone would blame me.

And in that moment and those that followed over the next couple days, I realized how beautiful I had become. All the wonderful things I had experienced and accomplished over the last eight years. The family I made for myself. And I realized I had not given myself enough credit nor enjoyed that enough. I was so wrapped up in my trauma that my amazing life and all its possibilities were passing me by.

This epiphany forced me to sit back and reminisce about all the POSITIVE things that happened over the last eight years. I was a beautiful, loving, caring, and strong woman who had been caring *for* and taking care *of* herself and thriving. I wasn't a failure, a mess, or trash to be thrown away. All those were negative things I carried around in this invisible backpack I felt I couldn't remove.

It was nice to know my parents were physically OK; I guess? But it became very clear that the past was the past. I couldn't go back in time and reconnect to this like it was before. Nor did I feel it was possible to build that type of relationship back up. That part of my life was over. I needed to forgive this and let it go and that didn't mean it was OK or that I wanted a child/parent relationship with them. It meant I forgave, allowing myself the opportunity to truly enjoy, appreciate and acknowledge that I am worthy of a great life; that I am an amazing person, and I am not as broken as all the negative voices led me to believe.

I couldn't move forward pretending this never happened or pretend I came from a different family, but I *could* choose my happiness instead of allowing my traumas to control me. And that is beautiful.

May 6, 2021
A note from my son:
". . . I understand, that's why I wanted to branch out to the people that were there for me. I'm always trying to be forgiving and not hold grudges. I've never wished ill intent for you or anyone in my life that might've done something I viewed as 'harmful'. Without you, I wouldn't be here, so I sincerely thank you for that. I appreciate you feeding me, taking me to school, getting me Pokémon cards, and all the other things that happened. I like to look back at the past sometimes in the apartment we used to live in back in Duarte. Makes me tear up sometimes. Just having that moment of simplicity and the occasional visiting grandparents on the weekend or during the holidays for school."

May 9, 2021
The moment arrived.

What started as a simple catching-up conversation with my son a few days before had turned into the first time I would see him after all these years apart. It unfolded in such a beautiful, unplanned way that I never could have planned any better. I purchased a super cheap airplane ticket out to California from early Saturday morning and a red eye flight on Sunday night to surprise one of my best friends for Mother's Day.

I told him I was coming for the weekend and asked if we could meet, and he hesitantly told me he would think about it and let me know. I tried my hardest not to get my hopes up as we had been in this place before and he changed his mind. But it was nearly impossible not to have my hopes up, praying it did not come crashing down again as it had before and if it did, I knew it wasn't personal. Our time would come and although it was OK to be disappointed, it wasn't worth harming myself or the progress I had made internally.

A permanent smile on my face, being in California with the possibility of seeing him, plus being with one of my best friends to unpack verbally the possible reunion, and I was beside myself. I was daydreaming of all the potential scenarios that could happen if we were to meet. *Would we hug? Would he laugh? Would I feel whole again? Would he see in my eyes how much I had missed him?* So many questions whirling around, just waiting for the opportunity to be answered.

The morning of May 9th arrived, and he reached out to say he was available to meet for lunch.

Immediately, a happiness overwhelmed me in a way I could never explain. The gate leading to the road of an emotional healing I could never fathom was now before me and all I had to do was start walking. I replayed all the words in my mind I had been waiting to say to him face-to-face for almost ten years.

As I got ready that day, an excitement and nervousness I had never felt before took over. Time stood still, and it seemed like forever until I could go. I wanted to be perfect for him. I wanted him to feel the same type of healing that I expected. I wanted both of us to heal for the better, even if it was only a tiny bit. I wanted it more for him than for myself by miles.

We agreed to meet at the restaurant that was our favorite to go-to as a little family of three growing up. This same spot also was the exact place I last saw him, which I felt brought even more of a climatic feeling to the entire moment.

I arrived and recognized him immediately. I never told him this, but the bench he was sitting on was the exact bench I sat on when I last saw him; except now he was waiting there for me, and I was walking toward him. We said hello, and I asked if it was OK to hug him; he obliged.

Have you ever heard of those stories where someone explains how their whole life flashed before their eyes and they relived everything in a cascading Rolodex of images? The moment I had my arms around him, that's what happened. The moment I had dreamed of all my life was happening, he was in my arms again. It sounds silly, but all I have ever wanted was to feel him again. I had searched all my life for a reason or way to feel whole again and always came up short. Through all the therapy and mindfulness, positive affirmations, and even speaking with my father again, everything had always fallen short, and I thought maybe that moment would never happen. Laying eyes on him and feeling my arms around him healed a place in my heart I thought would be broken forever.

We both moved with awkwardness and nervousness as we tried to navigate this interaction.

Settling at our table and ordering drinks, we exchanged common pleasantries.

After we ordered, I opened up and laid my soul bare in the most heartful apology ever to escape my soul. All the words I waited years to express to him. Taking accountabilities for all the things out of my control and within. I tried my hardest to portray the pain, guilt, and remorse that lives in my heart and to help him understand the things that happened, and things might not always be what they seem. Although the deepest reasoning behind what happened was beyond my control and without fault of my own, it did not change the fact that there was pain in his heart stemming from me and I, for that, took full accountability.

Tears came to my eyes, and his as well, in a moment that will forever replay in my mind. He accepted my apology and nothing, and I mean nothing, would ever surpass that moment.

For the next two hours, we played catch up. He filled me in on all the difficulties of the rest of his childhood and teen years. My heart broke many times after hearing his story. That he was ever in such a dark place, and I couldn't be there for him. But hearing how he was now and the road he was on to make a good life for himself made me so proud of him. He could have escaped down a deep, dark road and tragically left this life, but instead he picked himself up and maintained such a forgiving and open attitude about life and those in it. He laid his heart out in forgiveness of others and tried to relay that same emotion to others in his life to show a good example of this spirit. For that, I will be forever proud of him, my son.

Hearing more details about his life also gave me a glimpse into the trauma his sister and he experienced and how I could not help but hold a level of responsibility for, even though this was not how I chose things to happen. My heart ached for the stories he shared. My heart fell with the heartbreak he shared and the ways his mother should have been there to prevent those things from happening to him. How my duty as a mother to protect him was taken and robbed from me and I could never retrieve those moments to make amends to how they played out in his life. That fact those moments were out of my hands meant nothing at the moment he shared them, since I was reliving those moments through the expressions on his face and in his eyes.

The situation occurring how it had overall made it impossible for me to prevent or heal those things for him, whether then or now. I was a familiar stranger to him. I had been absent for so many years; it was impossible for me to swoop in and be a mother. I wanted to lay my life down to heal all his hurt places and insecurities and erase them from his very being. That was not an option. This was a trauma and a relationship I could never FIX. It will never be OK. I could grow and heal from here and now, but I could never go back in time and prevent it. Never. We both would just hope and try to find a way to navigate this to move forward.

I will spare many details of our conversation as I feel it should stay between us and our moment together, but not a day goes by that I don't replay it in my mind. Not a day that I don't see him sitting in that chair looking at me and us trying to create a space of healing. Not a day that all the daydreaming I had done over the years finally had a true photographic moment in my mind.

A true beginning for us to move forward, heal, and start a new journey being a part of each other's lives.

I thank God every day for bringing me that moment when he and I were truly ready to hold and accept it with the delicacy and open heartedness it deserved and needed. My "one day closer" came to a beautiful fruition beyond any way I could have imagined it happening.

That day before I met up with him, I texted my pastor's wife, with whom I had become close with as well, and told her, "Let Lee know I am going to see him." She told me his response was, "One day closer."

I thank all of you, my true family, for all the support I received over the years by my side, unwavering in this journey.

I thank the universe for giving me my children to bring into this world and love, even if it is from afar.

And I thank myself for continuing to heal and give myself grace and understanding every day for the roads ahead and what life will bring for us.

And finally, I am grateful for all the bumps in the road that have led me, led us all to this moment.

Everyone has a story, and this one is mine. I love my story. Love your story and make it your greatest accomplishment. Celebrate your trials and celebrate your successes. Celebrate realizing you made your way out of exile, you survived the hoax, and you came out better for it.

.

EPILOGUE

If I could go back and do it all again, I would because it brought me here and made me, *me*.

NO.

I am *me* because of the hard work I put in and the time I spent healing THAT'S what had made *me*, ME.

I refuse to give the power to trauma; it doesn't deserve it and it doesn't deserve any ounce of positive connotation in my life.

My trauma will never heal, I will forever search for the feeling I had with my family. I will forever search for myself in other people, and you know why? Because I am not perfect and that's OK.

Don't be afraid to allow yourself grace and compassion and allow yourself to fall short. It happens. We all do and you're not the exception to it. But what I do have now are more tools to help me through this. More affirmations to remind me how amazing I am, better connections with people who support this and encourage it and love me through it.

This is not about learning from my mistakes; this is about hearing another person make the same mistakes as you, so you don't feel you're the only person who has made or is making them.

This also isn't specific to just Jehovah's Witnesses. This is just my story and my experience. Maybe you will see a little of yourself in these pages for whatever mountain you're climbing or devil you're fighting.

Some days are good, and some days are bad; I really try my best to be positive and understand that I made it out on the other side, and I am in a better place now. I have been able to experience so many wonderful things and wonderful people since leaving that I never would have had I stayed indoctrinated in a cult.

I am an amazing person, a beautiful friend.

There are also many amazing things that happened in my life growing up when I was in the cult and that's OK to love, too.

And yes, I finally found a love that isn't built on toxic connection and searching for validation.

I feel so empowered, brave. It made me realize how amazing my life is, how much I've accomplished, and how far I've come as a human being.

I am here and healthy and able to share a small glimpse of my story, my life, in the hope to share with others that they are not alone. I share the scary thoughts and stories that others may not say out loud so when you read these words it brings you comfort you are not the only one who thinks or feels this way.

You are not your diagnosis. You can live your life. Recovering from a cult is possible and you are worth it, and you have so many other wonderful things to look forward to.

I love you Ding.

Born and raised in Southern California, Pony Jean has always had an affinity for books and writing. Growing up in a cult and being a survivor of religious trauma has moved her to become a mental health warrior sharing her story for others to connect with.

Pony Jean currently resides in Nashville, Tennessee working in the hospitality industry. In her free time, she enjoys reading, watching documentaries, hot yoga, and spending time with those close to her.

HISTORY OF TREATMENT

Pony Parker AKA ████████, Psychotherapy Treatment Report

Prepared by: Jillian Wendelin LMFT

May 30th, 2021

Client began treatment with Jillian Wendelin on 10/16/14. Jillian Wendelin was a licensed intern at the time and was under the supervision of Marj Buchholz LMFT. Treatment was sporadic as the client needed and at times there were financial challenges with attendance.

Upon intake client presented with stress and anxiety after a recent break up. Client presented with a flat affect and a sense of humor that felt to the clinician like a very effective coping skill for some serious pain in her life. The client initially touched on her upbringing as a Jehovah's Witness and losing contact with her family and children and leaving the church, but the clinical focus was on her current circumstances to start.

She reported that her ex was still "harassing her" over text. She reported having called the police to report the harassment and that he had left her with all the bills for where they were living. Client reported having moved from her home in California to Las Vegas to live with him. ████ left the session open to give a call when she felt in need of another session.

████ returned to therapy in January of 2015. She reported that she and her ex had decided to live together again after last session to share the bills and get back on her feet. She reported it not going well. They had been in a back-and-forth pattern for some time, but the client reported to be fully done with him. She and Jillian spoke about the possibility of people with narcissistic characteristics wanting to be involved with her when she might appear vulnerable.

A few months later client reported having read some books on narcissism that she found incredibly helpful, painful, but helpful. Client reported "feeling dumb" for letting herself get into various relationships with people who might have had these qualities.

The client returned to therapy after 6 months having felt really triggered because it "had been one year since she had seen my family or my kids." She reported dreaming about her children, ████████, and wanted to start the process up in court again to hopefully get to see them again. She wanted to figure out if the deep pain she felt was "grief or is it meant to motivate me to go back to court and fight."

On 9/3/15 ████ reported needing to see a student for a while so that she could afford therapy. Students were less costly than interns and there were students at the center who could join for a session and take over her case. Judith Sandora would be the therapist taking over her case, she joined the session on 9/22/15. She explained how she had lost custody of her children for the first time. The client reported feeling very betrayed by her family and misunderstood by the court. The client reported being involved with someone who she did not know was ████████████████████████████ and somehow the family and court found out and that combined with the alcohol use (which the client stated was only social) it was creating a stressful situation for her children. "I felt so unsure, and I wanted it to stop for my kids" she stated. So, she chose to stop fighting to protect her children.

Client returned to Jillian's care on 6/2/16 reporting a big jump in her anxiety and pervasive guilt. She had been dating someone new and realized they were in line with some of the same relationship choices she had made in the past, that thread of narcissistic qualities.

Client continued consistently in therapy for 3 months dealing with at times excessive tearfulness and at other times really heightened anxiety, and PTSD symptoms. Therapist used mindfulness training, CBT, and psychoeducation which did seem to help. ██████ was not able to continue treatment.

About a year later ██████ contacted Jillian over email to say that she had moved to Tennessee and had found a therapist, they did a release of information so that she and the new therapist could speak and hopefully help ██████ transition easier into treatment with the new therapist.

Jillian found the client to be delightfully funny and incredibly persistent even in the midst of incredibly difficulty and hoped that her amazing strengths would keep her stepping towards a healthier life.

Pony Parker aka ▇▇▇▇▇▇▇, Psychotherapy Treatment Report

Prepared by: Sarah Rodgers, LMFT, RDT

April 9, 2021

Client began treatment on 5/14/2018 with intern Lauren Lewallen, under supervision of Sarah Rodgers, LMFT. On initial intake paperwork, client described presenting issues including having limited local support, "no relationship with family", family history of anxiety, issues with eating infrequently and low appetite, a "strong tendency to date narcissists", and circled "Yes" in response to a question about history of trauma. In response to the question regarding use of alcohol and frequency of consumption, client wrote, "Yes and often."

In intake session with intern therapist Lauren Lewallen, whom ct saw for a short time (5/14/2018-6/4/2018) before transferring to work with Sarah Rodgers, LMFT, (beginning 6/18/2018) client described being "disowned" by her family 5 years prior. Client described family relationship issues and both romantic and platonic relationship issues, including history of physical abuse, such as having head slammed into a car, being cheated on, "leaving before someone can leave me", engaging in relationships with "narcissists", and being frequently blamed, yelled at unfairly. Client described symptoms including frequent inappropriate guilt, isolation, "no emotion" or feeling numb, anxiety and sadness. Strengths and social supports noted included church, career in hair, friends, and reading willingness to learn.

In initial sessions with Lauren, client described further symptoms: symptoms of trauma such as having vivid bad dreams about past relationships; symptoms of anxiety, for example worry and catastrophic thoughts about the risk of falling back into old patterns socially; and identified limiting internalized beliefs regarding interpersonal relationships and self, such as naming needs for control and avoidance of vulnerability. Client shared more about unhealthy family dynamics and history, including sexualized behavior by brother that was minimized and ignored, parents who did not look out for client's safety or wellbeing related to this issue, and being invalidated and gaslit in family of origin. Ct described having a bad relationship with father. Client recounted turbulent phases of late teens and early 20's including being married at 18, kicked out of the house because of pregnancy, and continued boundary issues with brother. Client shared that family members specifically made statements against client that significantly impacted client losing custody.

Client would describe all of these significant relationships and events with little to no affect, demonstrating disconnection and possible dissociation, an indication of lack of healthy integration of these events.

As first sessions went on, more symptoms of trauma were observed, including triggers for bad feelings (anxious or depressive), persistent negative or disturbing thoughts and inability to control thoughts, dissociation, tightness in chest, lack of self-worth (ie "I don't feel good enough for anyone"), and continued sadness. Client was reporting intrusive feelings and reminders of traumatic past events that were manifesting in a number of ways, both relational and mood, as well as physiological symptoms including chest tightness and an inability to physically relax. Ct at one point stated, "I don't relax."

Ct began working w/ Sarah Rodgers, LMFT in early July, 2018 to do EMDR on trauma, specifically the Negative Cognition "I am a failure". However, after identifying the EMDR target and establishing EMDR Safe Space, treatment did not proceed to EMDR processing phase because client reported higher activation and increased anxiety symptoms in the two following sessions. Client was exhibiting high anxiety, increased alcohol consumption, increased isolation, frustration, racing heart, chest tightness and body stress. Tp attempted to support ct with EMD to decrease physiological activation level, but ct did not respond well and reported finding the intervention to be unhelpful and somewhat agitating. Client and Tp discussed seeking medical evaluation immediately, as client's physical symptoms of chest tightness, racing heart and muscle tension had persisted for 4 days straight. Client did seek medical support.

Client was prescribed Klonopin and Celexa and at next appointment on 7 30 2018 ct was calmer and made hopeful statements about use of Celexa. After another week, on 8 6 2018, ct had decreased use of Klonopin and was reporting insomnia issues. Ct was not drinking because of medication and began attending AA meetings, reporting this was the longest stretch of time ct had been sober since she was pregnant. Ct demonstrated more interest in engaging in healthy habits and activities.

With sobriety, psychiatric medication compliance, and support of AA (and CoDA and NA) community, ct reported decreased insomnia, increased energy, more positive mood, and less ruminative anxious thoughts, stating, "I feel amazing." Ct was more able to acknowledge the depth of the role of ct's alcohol use in regards to family and custody issues, and to acknowledge her own addictive behaviors, like hiding alcohol in her room.

Ct continued to report challenges in personal relationships including: challenges with trusting herself, anticipating invalidation or being mis-perceived by others, choosing "the wrong person", and becoming hyper-focused on changing another's mind, even if the relationship has ended. These are all potential symptoms of client's complex relational trauma experiences.

Ct demonstrated similar strong anxious reaction to challenges in work relationships, reporting rumination, anxiety, and strong upset caused by feeling others are attacking her character. Ct exhibited tendency for over-controlling as a way to manage these emotional states and relationships. Ct and therapist spent time in sessions discussing discernment and building ct's abilities for building healthier relationships, as well as validating ct's own experiences and supporting healthier boundaries, while building skills to support managing anxiety.

Ct began to extricate herself from unhealthy personal and professional relationships, demonstrating more assertiveness around healthy boundaries, increased sense of self-worth, and investment in self-care and wellbeing. Ct also began to make more active choices to build positive social supports and engagement, including getting an AA Sponsor, reconnecting with friends who are also on a healing path, and becoming more involved in church, as well as building supportive connections with other shunned former members of ct's family's religion (former Jehova's Witnesses).

Ct began to initiate review of her life story thus far, sharing in session about various past experiences and phases of life, including recognizing influence of religion and parents' values, unhealthy patterns learned from early relationships, the impact on ct's sense of self and worth, violating or inappropriate experiences, and demonstrated insight and recognition about how she has grown and changed through these experiences. Client was more fair and kind to herself and less disconnected emotionally.

As client began to connect more with her experience, she continued to demonstrate some symptoms of PTSD/complex trauma including dreams about past upsetting experiences, inappropriate self-criticism, feeling "defective", inappropriate personal responsibility, and a perception there is "something wrong with me." The overall themes of perceiving self as flawed and unworthy, as related to experiences in family of origin, continued to be present. Ct also demonstrated a deeper understanding and recognition of her religious trauma as well as complex relational trauma as she opened up to herself and others more, including opening up more with therapist. Client invested time and energy into taking on a role of support for others, citing helping others as very meaningful and important for her, both by being more involved in church and being more active with ex-Witness community. Tp observed that helping others seemed to help client have a more positive sense of self, as well as help her focus and be positively motivated.

When ct faced the health issue of a problematic growth in her chin and needed to have procedure to address this, ct's sadness about isolation from her family came to the fore. Ct demonstrated frustration that she couldn't experience more healthy support. Again, ct made statements about how important it was for her to help others.

In June, 2019, ct reported experiencing sx of delayed alcohol withdrawal and seeking psychiatric support for these symptoms, continuing to demonstrate increased capacity for assertiveness and ability to meet her own needs, as well as increased investment in her own well-being.

While ct had previously reported instanced of increased ability to redirect anxiety, decrease impact of overthinking, and decrease self-criticism, client disclosed that she was still struggling with anxiety symptoms and that her meds were not actually working effectively, as confirmed by genetic testing. Ct reported having had physical anxiety symptoms since February as well as poor short-term memory, and also reported increased tearfulness and emotional lability. Ct changed to Zoloft and continued to be engaged in healthy habits (ie exercise) and healthy social and community engagement (ie serving at church).

Ct had recently reconnected with her children and was energetic about seeing photos, hearing updates, and made positive statements about the potential for those relationships. Ct took a break from therapy to deal with health issues and recovery from procedures. Tp did not hear from ct again until ct was in rehab, when ct reached out briefly. Despite being part of original discharge plan, Tp and ct did not resume working together.

TrustPoint
HOSPITAL

1009 N Thompson Ln.

Murfreesboro, TN 37129

615-962-6171 (P)

615-962-6188 (F)

December 2nd, 2019

To Whom It May Concern:

██████████ DOB: ████████ was admitted to TrustPoint Hospital on 11/22/2019 and discharged on 12/2/2019. ██████ may return to work with zero restrictions on 12/9/19 or sooner if she should decide she is ready. If you have any questions or if additional documentation is needed please give me a call at 615-962-6171.

MR#: 000204282
Hosp #: 0308615
DOB▮▮▮▮▮▮▮▮
Admit Date: 11/22/2019
Observation Date/Time: 11/22/2019 5:31:00P

HISTORY AND PHYSICAL EXAMINATION

DATE OF ADMISSION: 11/22/2019

ADMISSION DIAGNOSIS:
Suicidal ideation.

HISTORY OF PRESENT ILLNESS:
▮▮▮▮▮▮▮▮ is a 37-year-old female who was taken to the Saint Thomas
Rutherford Hospital Emergency Department on 11/21/2019, with a complaint of
suicidal ideation for over 2 weeks. The patient reports that she attempted to
drink until she "dies." She had been sober for 15 months on her own, no prior
residential treatment for alcohol use, but relapsed 2 weeks ago, has since been
drinking 1 to 2 bottles of wine daily. She attributes her stressors to lack of
relationship with her 2 children, ages 16 and 18, who are with their father, and a
strained relationship with her parents and entire family due to her refusal to be
part of the Jehovah's Witness section of Christianity. She states that she goes
to church, but for 30 years of her life she was fully active in the Jehovah's
Witness religion, when she decided to quit approximately 6 years ago. Her
entire family including her husband and children disowned her. Now, she
endorses a feeling of loneliness, hopelessness, helplessness, and being
extremely overwhelmed for the past few months. She takes sertraline 100 mg
and feels like it does not help with her depression. Also has been prescribed
Klonopin for generalized anxiety disorder, but barely takes it. During my
interview with ▮▮▮▮▮▮▮ she cried multiple times during the interview. She
feels like nobody understands that it is a situational depression and medication
is not fixing it. However, she is not willing to return back to the Jehovah's
Witness faith so that her family would accept her. Hence, she feels that she is
"lost." After medical clearance, she was deemed to be medically stable and was
referred to TrustPoint for involuntary inpatient psychiatric admission.
Currently, she denies suicidal ideation, homicidal ideation, auditory
hallucination, or visual hallucinations. Furthermore, she denies headache,
dizziness, chest pain, visual disturbances, neck pain, abdominal pain, nausea,
vomiting, diarrhea, constipation, urinary symptoms, fever, chills and body
aches.

REVIEW OF SYSTEMS:
One through 12 have been reviewed, otherwise negative except as noted in the
HPI.

MEDICAL HISTORY:
Denies.

PSYCHIATRIC HISTORY:
Major depressive disorder.
Generalized anxiety disorder.

HOME MEDICATIONS:
Sertraline 100 mg daily.
Klonopin 0.5 mg daily as needed.

ALLERGIES:
Hydrocodone.

Command Health History and Physical

MR#: 000204282
Hosp #: 0308615
DOB: ███████
Admit Date: 11/22/2019
Observation Date/Time: 11/22/2019 5:31:00P

SOCIAL HISTORY:
The patient is single, has 2 children, ages 18 and 16, who are with her ex-husband. Quit smoking 15 months ago. Prior to that, had about a 2-pack-year smoking history. She reports that she had extensive alcohol use, started drinking at age of 15, quit drinking approximately 15 months ago, but relapsed 2 weeks ago and has since been drinking on a daily basis. Further details as stated in the HPI. Denies illicit drug use. She works full-time as a technician in a psychiatric facility.

FAMILY HISTORY:
Unknown to patient due to strained relationship.

PHYSICAL EXAMINATION:
GENERAL: Pleasant, cooperative, well developed, well nourished, no acute distress.
VITAL SIGNS: Temperature 98.3, blood pressure 93/61, pulse 73, respirations 14, oxygen saturation 98%. Height 69 inches, weight 145.4 pounds.
HEENT: Normocephalic and atraumatic. Pupils are equal and reactive to light and accommodation. Oral mucosa is moist without lesion. Nasal passages patent.
NECK: Supple without lymphadenopathy or thyromegaly. Trachea is midline.
CARDIOVASCULAR: Regular rate and rhythm. Normal S1, S2. No murmurs, JVD, or gallops appreciated.
RESPIRATORY: Clear bilaterally to auscultation. Respirations are even and nonlabored.
ABDOMEN: Soft, nondistended, nontender. Normoactive bowel sounds in all quadrants.
EXTREMITIES: She has 2+ pulses in all extremities. No edema, clubbing, or cyanosis appreciated.
SKIN: Warm, dry, without lesions.
NEUROLOGICAL EXAMINATION OF CRANIAL NERVES: Cranial Nerve I. Olfactory: Demonstrates ability to identify familiar odors.
Cranial Nerve II. Optical: Demonstrates gross visual acuity.
Cranial Nerve III. Oculomotor: Extraocular muscle movements have a normal upward and medial gaze. Normal accommodation.
Cranial Nerve IV. Trochlear: Extraocular muscle movements have a normal downward gaze.
Cranial Nerve V. Trigeminal: Demonstrates facial sensation.
Cranial Nerve VI. Abducens: Extraocular muscle movements have a normal lateral gaze.
Cranial Nerve VII. Facial: Demonstrates use of facial muscles.
Cranial Nerve VIII. Auditory: Hears conversational voice.
Cranial Nerve IX - X: Glossopharyngeal and Vagus: Normal palate elevation, phonation and gag reflex.
Cranial Nerve XI. Spinal Accessory: Bilaterally symmetrical shoulder shrug strength.
Cranial Nerve XII. Hypoglossal: Normal tongue protrusion.
PSYCHIATRIC: Alert and fully oriented. Speech is intact. Tearful throughout the exam.

DIAGNOSTIC STUDIES:
The following labs were done at the previous facility on 11/21/2019: Sodium

Command Health History and Physical

MR#: 000204282
Hosp #: 0308615
DOB:
Admit Date: 11/22/2019
Observation Date/Time: 11/22/2019 5:31:00P

140, potassium 3.7, chloride 111, CO2 of 21, BUN 17, creatinine 0.7, creatinine clearance 114.5, glucose 104, calcium 8.8, total protein 6.0, albumin 3.9, bilirubin total 0.6, alkaline phosphatase 49, AST 16, ALT 13, anion gap 8, bilirubin direct 0.2, lipase 28. Blood alcohol less than 10 mg/dL. Salicylate less than 1.8 mg/dL. UDS positive for benzodiazepines only. Tylenol less than 10 mcg/dL. WBC 5.5, RBC 3.75, hemoglobin 11.7, hematocrit 36.5, RDW 11.9, platelets 200,000.

Pending labs are hemoglobin A1c, lipid panel, and TSH, as well as a pregnancy test.

ASSESSMENT AND PLAN:

Suicidal ideation in a patient with history of major depressive disorder and generalized anxiety disorder. Defer to Psychiatry.

Deep venous thrombosis prophylaxis. Encourage the patient to ambulate the halls.

Substance use disorder secondary to alcohol use. Cessation counseling has been provided to the patient. Last drink was over 24 hours and the patient exhibits no signs and symptoms of withdrawal. We will continue to monitor the patient.

DISPOSITION:

Inpatient.

Time spent 45 minutes.

Electronically Signed - 11/26/2019 09:00 PM

Electronically Signed - 12/01/2019 08:34 AM

GT/mt/71842767

DD: 11/22/2019 05:31 P.M.
DT: 11/22/2019 07:36 P.M.

Psychiatric Evaluation

Chief Complaint (in patient's own words)

DATE OF SERVICE: 11/22/19

" I don't care"

Events that led client to seek treatment at this time. (Intake)

The pt is a 37 yr old SCF, with a hx of depression, anxiety, PTSD and alcohol abuse, presented to St. Thomas West Hospital ER via walk-in reporting SI and that she attempted suicide the previous night by "drinking until I didn't wake up." The pt reported feeling increasingly suicidal over the past several days. She also reported drinking alcohol for the past two weeks after 15 yrs sobriety. The pt states she has been through a lot this year and four people she was close to o has died within the past three months. The pt said she was raised as a Jehovah's Witness and when she decided to leave the faith, she was shunned by her family and they ontained full custody of the pt's two children. She has not seen or spoken to her children in six years. The pt is prescribed Sertraline 100 mg daily and Clonazepam .5mg nightly/PRN. The pt reported med compliance. UDS positive for barbiturates and BAL was negative. The pt is unable to contract for safety and was admitted for treatment

What happened in last 72 hrs that led to Precipitating Crisis/Chief Complaint? (Intake)

SA on 11/20/2019 by alcohol poisoning and ongoing SI without a clear plan.

History of Present Illness

This is patient's first psychiatric hospitalization for worsening depression and suicidal thoughts . In fact she tried to to end her life 2 days ago by alcohol poisoning.
Pt reports severe depression, hopelessness, helplessness and worthlessness. Pt says her family has disowned her. Struggling to deal with the loss from multiple deaths She is having difficulty in maintaining her job and now feeling even more devastated due to relapsing on alcohol after 15 months of sobriety. She has started working in MTMHI a month ago. This is her 5 th job in past 15 months.
She carries a diagnosis of PTSD PTSD from childhood issues but does not want to talk about it at present.

Past Psychiatric History (To include prior precipitating factors, past diagnoses, course of treatment, past hospitalization or harm attempts)

None
No history of Inpatoent substance abuse treatment. Attends AA meetings

Drug/Alcohol Abuse History (To include drugs of choice, patterns of use treatment history)

Alcohol mainly; drinking 1-2 bottles of wine /day for past 2 weeks

Past or present medical conditions

Yes

Depression, anxiety, PTSD

Allergy Comments	Type	Reaction	Severity	Date	Code	System
REPRODNone	Drug Allergy					

Psychiatric Evaluation

MR#: 000204282
Hosp #: 0308615
DOB ████████
Admit Date: 11/22/2019
Observation Date/Time: 11/23/2019 2:51:00P

Social History (To include educational level, vocational/occupational/employment history/status, interpersonal relationships and supports)	Currently employed as a psych tech in MTMH! Full time student Receives out patient psychiatric treatment at Alleviant Health Centers
Family History (To include any psychiatric or substance history within the family)	Father and brother suffer from Depression and social anxiety Alcoholism runs in the family.

Description Indication	Brand	Dose	Route	Frequency	PRN
----------	-----	----	-----	---------	---
SERTRALINE Oral 100 mg TAB	Zoloft	100 mg	PO	2100	

Constitutional Review

Systolic	124 mmHg
Diastolic	72 mmHg
Pulse	84 beats/min
Temperature	98.1 °F Oral
Height	69 in
Weight	145.4 lb
Respirations	16 Resp/Min

Psychiatric Evaluation

Musculoskeletal Examination

Abnormal/Involuntary Movements	None
Strength	Greater than antigravity (> 3/5) in all extremities
Muscle Tone	No impairment
Gait	Grossly normal
Station	Grossly normal

Mental Status Examination

General Appearance	Casual
Speech/Language	Spontaneous
Attitude/Behavior	Cooperative and Withdrawn
Mood	Anxious and Depressed
Affect	Blunted and tearful
Orientation	Time, Place, Person and Situation
Thought Content	WNL
Suicidal	Plan

Psychiatric Evaluation

To drink excessive amount of alcol

Homicidal	Patient Denies
Perception	WNL
Thought Process	Goal-oriented
Concentration/Attention Span	WNL
How Tested/Assessed?	"Per Observation and interview with the patient"
Recent Memory	WNL
How Tested/Assessed? (3 out of 3 in 3 minutes)	2 out of 3
Remote Memory	WNL
How Tested/Assessed?	"Past events, as relates history"
Intelligence	Average
How Tested/Assessed?	Based on history
Judgment	Poor
How Tested/Assessed?	Per patient's behavior/history of present illness
Insight	Poor

Psychiatric Evaluation

How Tested/Assessed?   Understanding severity of illness/history of present illness

Mental Status Examination

Diagnosis Code	System	Class	Type	Priority	Date
Ethanol dependence, 11/23/2019 F10.20 ICD-10 uncomplicated		Behavioral Health	Admitting	Primary Diagnosis	
Major depressive disorder, 11/23/2019 F33.2 ICD-10 recurrent severe without psychotic features		Behavioral Health	Admitting	Primary Diagnosis	
Post-traumatic stress 11/23/2019 F43.12 ICD-10 disorder, chronic		Behavioral Health	Admitting	Secondary Diagnosis	

Patient Strengths (Check 2 or more)   Able to vocalize needs and Access to healthcare

Please elaborate on patient's strenghts providing detail or explanation   N/A

Patient Limitations   Lack of Social Supports and Being away from children

Initial Plan of Care
Admit on commitment status
Thorough medical eval to R/O medical possibilities
Medication stabilization
SW to obtain collateral information
Re start home meds and increase Sertraline
Attend groups

Estimated Length of Stay (Number of days anticipated)   7

Initial Discharge Plan   Home

Prognosis   Fair

Justification for Hospitalization

Psychiatric Evaluation

Inpatient or Partial? **Inpatient**

Inpatient Hospitalization "Dangerous to self, others or property with need for controlled environment" and Failure of treatment at a lower level of care

Psychiatrist Signature Signed by ████████ at 11/23/2019 15:21

Charges from this Assessment

Choose All Charges that Apply **Charge with Medical Services**

90792 - Psychiatric Diagnostic Evaluation with medical services 1

Discharge Summary-Behavioral Unit

Identifying Information	37yo Caucasian female
Chief Complaint	"pretty good"
Reason for Hospitalization (to include history of present illness)	
Events that led client to seek treatment at this time	Per previous note: The pt is a 37 yr old SCF, with a hx of depression, anxiety, PTSD and alcohol abuse, presented to St. Thomas West Hospital ER via walk-in reporting SI and that she attempted suicide the previous night by "drinking until I didn't wake up." The pt reported feeling increasingly suicidal over the past several days. She also reported drinking alcohol for the past two weeks after 15 yrs sobriety. The pt states she has been through a lot this year and four people she was close to o has died within the past three months. The pt said she was raised as a Jehovah's Witness and when she decided to leave the faith, she was shunned by her family and they ontained full custody of the pt's two children. She has not seen or spoken to her children in six years. The pt is prescribed Sertraline 100 mg daily and Clonazepam .5mg nightly/PRN. The pt reported med compliance. UDS positive for barbiturates and BAL was negative. The pt is unable to contract for safety and was admitted for treatment
What happened in the last 72 hours that led to Precipitating Crisis/Chief Complaint?	Per previous note: SA on 11/20/2019 by alcohol poisoning and ongoing SI without a clear plan.
Past Psychiatric History	Per previous note: None No history of Inpatoent substance abuse treatment. Attends AA meetings
Course of Treatment	Patient was admitted on commitment status. Thorough medical evaluation was done by the consulting medical service to r/o medical possibilities. Patient was monitored on suicidal and behavioral precautions. Pt was started was switched from zoloft to lexapro to target mood instability. Propranolol was added to address anxiety. She made improvement in mood. She tolerated medications well. She was hopeful and motivated prior to d/c. She plans to attend A&D program upon d/c. She denied SI prior to d/c.
Physical/Medical Condition on Discharge	stable
Functional Condition on Discharge	stable

Examination

Discharge Summary-Behavioral Unit

MR#: 000204282
Hosp #. 0308615
DOB:
Admit Date: 11/22/2019
Observation Date/Time: 12/2/2019 2:28:00PM

General Appearance	Well-groomed
Psychomotor Behavioral	WNL
Speech	Spontaneous
Attitude	Cooperative
Mood	Euthymic
Affect	Full Range
Orientation	Time, Place, Person and Situation
Thought Content	WNL
Risk Factors	No Risk Factors
Perception	WNL
Thought Process	Goal-Oriented
Concentration/Attention	WNL
How Tested/Assessed	Per Observation and interview with the patient
Recent Memory	WNL
How Tested/Assessed: out of 3 in 3 minutes	3 out of 3

Discharge Summary-Behavioral Unit

MR#: 000204282
Hosp #: 0308615
DOB: █████████
Admit Date: 11/22/2019
Observation Date/Time: 12/2/2019 2:28:00PM

Remote Memory	WNL
How Tested/Assessed	Past events, as relates history
Intelligence	Average
How Tested/Assessed	Based on history; based on vocab, syntax, grammar, content
Judgment	Fair
How Tested/Assessed	Per patient's behavior
Insight	Fair
How Tested/Assessed	Understanding severity of illness

Diagnosis Code	System	Class	Type	Priority	Date
─────────		─────	────	────────	────
Differential gastric stomatitis with exanthem					
Alcohol dependence, 11/22/2019 F10.20 ICD-10 uncomplicated		Behavioral Health	Admitting	Primary Diagnosis	
Major depressive disorder, 11/22/2019 F33.2 ICD-10 recurrent severe without psychotic features		Behavioral Health	Admitting	Primary Diagnosis	
Post-traumatic stress 11/22/2019 F43.12 ICD-10 disorder, chronic		Behavioral Health	Admitting	Secondary Diagnosis	

Discharge Summary-Behavioral Unit

MR#: 000204282
Hosp #: 0308615
DOB: ████████████
Admit Date: 11/22/2019
Observation Date/Time: 12/2/2019 2:28:00PM

Description Indication	Brand	Dose	Route	Frequency	PRN
------------	-----	----	-----	----------	---
ARIPIPRAZOLe Oral 2 mg TAB	Ability	2 mg	PO	DAILY	Mood
escitalopram 5 mg TAB Depression	Lexapro	15 mg	PO	HS	
gabapentin Oral 100 mg CAP Anxiety	Neurontin	200 mg	PO	TID	
prazosin 2 mg CAP nightmares	Minipress	2 mg	PO	HS	
propranolol Oral 10 mg TAB Anxiety	Inderal	10 mg	PO	TID	

Recommendations/Followup/Aftercare

pt to d/c to MLRC in Burns, TN. Will have f/u care there.

Signatures

Physician or Physician Extender Signature

Signed by ███████████████ at 12/02/2019 14:36

Physician Cosignature

Signed by ███████████████ at 01/23/2020 16:31

Charges from this Assessment

Choose All Charges that Apply

Hospital Discharge Day Management; 30 Minutes Or Less

99238 - Hospital Discharge Day Management; 30 Minutes Or Less

1

cumberland heights

1/02/2020

████ "Pony" ████
████████████

Re: **Presence in Treatment**

Patient: ████ "Pony" ████

- DOB: ████████

Admitted Inpatient: 12/05/2019
Regular Discharge: 1/02/2020

Dear ████

This letter will confirm that you were treated at Cumberland Heights (current TDMHSAS license #L00000024084) for a substance use disorder. Upon discharge you received a continuing care plan for ongoing recovery support.

Sincerely,

████████████

Case Manager, Women's Program
Cumberland Heights

Cumberland Heights
8283 River Road Pike
Nashville, TN 37209
EIN: -
Phone: 615-356-2700
Fax: 615-432-3021

Orders - Current Medications

Current Medications

Active Orders

No Active Orders

Created Orders

No Created Orders

Expired Orders

Medications	Comments	Start On	Ordered By	Entered By
Escitalopram (Oral Pill) - Escitalopram 5 MG Oral Tablet 3 tabs PO At hours of sleep, 60. Refill: 0	Depression/Anxiety	2019-12-05	███████	███████
VISTARIL (Oral Pill) - Hydroxyzine Pamoate 50 MG Oral Capsule 1 PO Now, 1. Refill:	anxiety	2019-12-08	███████	███████
zyprexa zydis 10mg 1 PO Now, 1. Refill:	anxiety/agitation	2019-12-09	███████	███████
wellbutrin xl 150mg 1 Once a day, 30. Refill:	depression	2019-12-17	███████	███████
latuda 60mg 1 PO At hours of sleep, 30. Refill:	mood stabilizer	2019-12-17	███████	███████
prazosin 3mg 1 PO At hours of sleep, 30. Refill:	ptsd	2019-12-16	███████	███████
gabapentin 800mg 1 PO At 15:00, 08:00, 21:30, 30. Refill:	mood stabilizer / anxiety	2019-12-17	███████	███████

Discontinued Orders

Medications	Comments	Start On	Ordered By	Entered By
aripiprazole 2 mg 1 tab PO Once a day, 60. Refill: 0	Depression	2019-12-06	███████	███████
Gabapentin (Oral Pill) - gabapentin 100 MG Oral Capsule 2 tabs PO At	Anxiety	2019-12-05	███████	███████

Cumberland Heights
8283 River Road Pike
Nashville, TN 37209
EIN: -
Phone: 615-356-2700
Fax: 615-432-3021

Medication	Indication	Date		
15:00, 21:30, 08:00, 60. Refill: 0			████	
Escitalopram (Oral Pill) - Escitalopram 5 MG Oral Tablet 3 tabs PO At hours of sleep, 60, Refill: 0		2019-12-05	████	████
Prazosin (Oral Pill) - Prazosin 2 MG Oral Capsule 1 tab PO At hours of sleep, 60, Refill: 0		2019-12-05	████	████
Propranolol (Oral Pill) - Propranolol Hydrochloride 10 MG Oral Tablet 1 tab PO At 08:00, 21:30, 15:00, 60, Refill: 0	Anxiety	2019-12-05	████	████
aripiprazole 2 mg 1 tab PO Once a day, 60, Refill: 0	Depression	2019-12-06	████	████
Prazosin (Oral Pill) - Prazosin 2 MG Oral Capsule 1 tab PO At hours of sleep, 60, Refill: 0	PTSD	2019-12-05	████	████
gabapentin 300mg 1 PO At 21:30, 08:00, 12:30, 30, Refill:	anxiety/agitation	2019-12-09	████	████
gabapentin 300mg 1 PO At 12:30, 08:00, 21:30, 30, Refill:	anxiety/agitation	2019-12-09	████	████
gabapentin 300mg 1 PO At 21:30, 08:00, 15:00, 30, Refill:	anxiety/agitation	2019-12-10	████	████
ABILIFY (Oral Pill) - aripiprazole 5 MG Oral Tablet 1 PO At 08:00, 30, Refill:	Depression	2019-12-12	████	████
prazosin 3mg 1 PO At hours of sleep, 30, Refill:	ptsd	2019-12-16	████	████
latuda 60mg 1 PO Once a day, 30, Refill:	mood stabilization	2019-12-16	████	████

Cumberland Heights
8283 River Road Pike
Nashville, TN 37209
EIN -
Phone: 615-356-2700
Fax: 615-432-3021

Diagnosis Reference Guide for 2019-12-05

Diagnosis Type: Primary

Substance Type: Alcohol

1. Substance is often taken in larger amounts and/or over a longer period than the patient intended. Yes

2. Persistent attempts or one or more unsuccessful efforts made to cut down or control substance use. Yes

3. A great deal of time is spent in activities necessary to obtain the substance, use the substance, or recover from effects. Yes

4. Craving or strong desire or urge to use the substance. Yes

5. Recurrent substance use resulting in a failure to fulfill major role obligations at work, school, or home. No

6. Continued substance use despite having persistent or recurrent social or interpersonal problem caused or exacerbated by the effects of the substance. No

7. Important social, occupational or recreational activities given up or reduced because of substance use. Yes

8. Recurrent substance use in situations in which it is physically hazardous. Yes

9. Substance use is continued despite knowledge of having a persistent or recurrent physical or psychological problem that is likely to have been caused or exacerbated by the substance. Yes

10. Tolerance, as defined by either of the following: a. Markedly increased amounts of the substance in order to achieve intoxication or desired effect; b. Markedly diminished effect with continued use of the same amount; No

11. Withdrawal, as manifested by either of the following: a. The characteristic withdrawal syndrome for the substance; b. The same (or a closely related) substance is taken to relieve or avoid withdrawal symptoms; Yes

Severity: Severe (6+ symptoms present)

Score 8.0

Preliminary Diagnosis for 2019-12-05

Diagnostic Codes	From	Until	Type
F1020 - Alcohol Use Disorder, Severe	2019-12-05		Primary
Z62820 - Parent-biological child conflict	2019-12-05		Other
Z62811 - Personal history of psychological abuse in childhood	2019-12-05		Tertiary
Z9149 - Other personal history of psychological trauma, not elsewhere classified	2019-12-05		Secondary

Assessment Summary for 2019-12-05

Assessment Summary Pt arrived for assessment voluntarily. Pt reports DOC as alcohol, with first use at age 13, and last use 11/20/19. Pt reports drinking 2 bottles of wine daily for the past six months. Pt reports coming to treatment because she wants to get sober. Pt reports history of prior treatment. Pt reports a history of attending 12 step recovery meetings. Pt reports reason for relapse ████████████ among other things contributing to a rough year. Pt does not present with withdrawal symptoms. Pt denies history of seizures. Pt reports history of DT's. Pt admits previous detox treatment.

This information has been disclosed to you for records protected by Federal and State confidentiality rules and laws (42 CFR Part 2, 45 CFR, HIPAA, and T.C.A. 33-3-104). The Federal and State Rules prohibit you from making any further disclosure of this information unless further

Cumberland Heights
8283 River Road Pike
Nashville, TN 37209
EIN: -
Phone: 615-356-2700
Fax: 615-432-3021

Pt reports mental health diagnosis of anxiety, depression, PTSD, and Borderline Personality Disorder. Pt reports current psychotropic medications and compliance with those medications. Pt. denies current SI,HI, or SIB but admits previous SI with two attempts, the last one being 11/20/19. Pt. appears anxious and depressed. Pt appears to lack judgment and insight at this time. Pt reports the reason for relapse is ███████████████. Pt admits history of trauma, as she left the cult she grew up in six years ago and her family disowned her and took her kids away from her. Pt. denies a history of sexual and physical abuse, but admits a history of emotional abuse growing up in a cult. Pt denies feeling out of control when angry or anxious. Pt reports being internally motivated for treatment by not wanting to feel how she feels. Pt reports being externally motivated for treatment by wanting to see her kids again.

Pt reports a history of blackouts, the last one being on 11/20/19 Pt admits to driving while intoxicated, the last time being July 2018. Pt denies history of DUI's. Pt denies engaging in activities that may be illegal to obtain drugs. Pt denies physical altercations. Pt denies other dangerous behaviors (falling, buying drugs in dangerous areas, loss of consciousness, injuries due to use.) Pt denies substance use has had physical effects. Pt admits to spending $112 per week on substance use. Pt reports funding substance use by working. Pt denies financial problems due to substance use. Pt denies having sold drugs to fund substance use. Pt. denies having stolen or pawned items to fund substance use. Pt reports history of 12 step recovery meetings. Pt reports a high level of participation. Pt denies having a sponsor. Pt admits history of working a step study program. Pt reports last working on step 12. Pt reports having a lot of sober support.

Pt reports currently living with roommate and reports living in current home for 8 months. Pt reports the intention to return to the same after treatment is completed. Pt denies that someone in the home uses substances. Pt denies substances are available in the home. Pt denies home life is stressful. Pt reports no children under the age of 18 living in the home. Pt reports friend (who she calls her sister) as primary relationship. Pt denies living with an abusive person. Pt denies verbal altercations and denies physical altercations in the home. Pt reports a non-existent relationship with family. Pt reports having many friends. Pt reports having 2 children who were taken from her by her family 6 six years ago when she left the cult. Pt reports that no one has asked Pt to stop using. Pt reports substance use has not affected family. Pt denies lying to family about substance use. Pt denies stealing from family to fund substance use. Pt reports a family history of mental illness - depression and anxiety on father's side. Pt reports family history of addiction - father is an alcoholic. Pt denies that primary social group is made up of substance users. Pt admits isolating frequently.

Pt reports being currently employed as a Psychiatric Technician. Pt reports having been with current employer for 3 months. Pt denies missing days of work in the last 30 days for reasons related to substance use. Pt denies job is in jeopardy. Pt. reports going to work hung over. Pt admits using while at work. Pt. denies having lost jobs due to substance use. Pt reports having a technical degree in cosmetology. Pt is currently attending school and denies problems at school due to substance use. Pt denies issues with reliable transportation or childcare. Pt reports substances are easily obtained in current community environment.

Treatment Recommendation for 2019-12-05

Level of care recommended: 3.5 - Residential

Treatment Recommendation: Recommending residential level of care with additional treatment recommendations and step-down recommendation to be determined by clinical staff.

Signatures

███████████████

████████████████
12/05/2019 01:48:37 PM

Cumberland Heights
8283 River Road Pike
Nashville, TN 37209
EIN: -
Phone: 615-356-2700
Fax: 615-432-3021

Nursing - Nursing Note

Nursing Note for 2019-12-08

Type: General

Nursing Note: Pt brought to medical by CA ████. Pt has SI without a plan. She has negative feelings associated with losing her children and general feelings of helplessness. She is inconsolable and crying. Completed suicide assessment and she has a 24 hour assessment due tomorrow. She had a suicide attempt 3 weeks ago by trying to drink herself to death, she was unsuccessful and was hospitalized before coming to CH. Spoke with patient at length about using the AA program to help cope with her difficulties including use of a higher power. Called oncall MD and received one time order for Vistaril 50mg for anxiety which was given along with Pt's night medications. Pt's mood slightly improved. She had no current plan to hurt herself, no HI. She still has SI but says she always has it. Pt agreed to reach out to staff if she feels more intense feelings or if she has a plan to hurt self. Pt was transferred back to women's cabin by CA ████.
████████

Signatures

████████████

12/08/2019 10:07:31 PM

Cumberland Heights
8283 River Road Pike
Nashville, TN 37209
EIN: -
Phone: 615-356-2700
Fax: 615-432-3021

Nursing - Nursing Note

Nursing Note for 2019-12-14

Type: General

Nursing Note. Pt presented to medical with severe anxiety and helplessness. CA present. Sat with patient and discussed her anxiety causes and solutions including medication, 12 steps, meditation and developing a more positive outlook on life. Asked her to speak with her counselor about her problems including traumatic issues. Pt received night meds and PRN Vistaril for anxiety. She was put on MD board for tomorrow.

▮▮▮▮▮▮

Signatures

12/14/2019 10:00:03 PM

Cumberland Heights
8283 River Road Pike
Nashville TN 37209
EIN: -
Phone: 615-356-2700
Fax: 615-432-3021

Medical - Initial Psychiatric Evaluation

Chief Complaint/History of Present Illness for 2019-12-09

Chief Complaint " I need help with my anxiety and depression."

History of Present Illness This is a 37 year old female presenting for evaluation and treatment of an alcohol use disorder. The patient gives a history of progressive alcohol abuse. She has been consuming up to two bottles of wine per evening. She has experienced alcohol induce blackouts but has no history of complicated withdrawals such as seizure activity or delirium tremors. She denies any illicit drug use prior to her current admission. The patient has a co-occurring history of depression and anxiety. She describes having chronic feeling of hopelessness accompanied by suicidal thoughts, she has been previously diagnosed with depression, anxiety, ptsd, and borderline personality disorder. While she has frequent thoughts of death and suicide. She denies specific plan or intent. She states that she a number of trauma related events in her life. These include being raised in a cult like environment and the separation from her children. She denies any history of psychosis. She reports she capable of participating with a safety plan while in treatment.

Psychiatric Review of Systems: for 2019-12-09

Depression

☐ Denies

☐ Mood Level Up

☑ Mood Level Down

☐ Mood Level Average

☐ Irritability

☐ Energy Level Up

☑ Energy Level Down

☐ Energy Level Good

☐ Anhedonia

☐ Excessive Guilt

☑ Poor Concentration

Depression Level (0-10) 8

If yes to any, describe

_____

Anxiety:

☐ Denies

☑ General

☐ Panic

☐ Obsessions

Cumberland Heights
8283 River Road Pike
Nashville, TN 37209
EIN -
Phone: 615-356-2700
Fax: 615-432-3021

Medical - Addiction Medicine Follow Up

Behavioral Diagnosis for 2019-12-20

Diagnostic Codes	From	Until	Type
F1020 - Alcohol Use Disorder, Severe	2019-12-06		Primary
F4310 - Post-traumatic stress disorder, unspecified	2019-12-06		Secondary
F603 - Borderline personality disorder	2019-12-06		Secondary
F419 - Anxiety disorder, unspecified	2019-12-09		Secondary

Medical Diagnosis for 2019-12-20

Diagnostic Codes

Vitals for 2019-12-20

Physical Exam Vitals	Time	Blood Pressure	Temperature	Pulse	Respirations	O2 Saturation	Height	Weight

Physician Note for 2019-12-20

Physician Note: feeling hopeless, "like I want to go to sleep and never wake up."

she reported passive SI at least for the past week

no plans for SI, commits to safety

anxiety better, but no change in depression

low energy

appetite good

sleeping well

affect of limited range, speech fluent, thoughts coherent

will cont current meds and monitor response

cont residential tx

Medication Assisted Treatment for 2019-12-20

Is the patient a candidate for medication assisted treatment? ○ Yes ○ No

Comments:

If yes, information given and discussed? ○ Yes ○ No

Comments:

Patient accepted MAT recommendation? ○ Yes ○ No

Comments:

Once stable, the activity level can be:

Vivitrol administered? ○ Yes ○ No

Cumberland Heights
8283 River Road Pike
Nashville, TN 37209
EIN: -
Phone: 615-356-2700
Fax: 615-432-3021

Diagnosis Reference Guide for 2019-12-06

Diagnosis Type: Primary

Substance Type: Alcohol

1. Substance is often taken in larger amounts and/or over a longer period than the patient intended. Yes

2. Persistent attempts or one or more unsuccessful efforts made to cut down or control substance use. Yes

3. A great deal of time is spent in activities necessary to obtain the substance, use the substance, or recover from effects. Yes

4. Craving or strong desire or urge to use the substance. Yes

5. Recurrent substance use resulting in a failure to fulfill major role obligations at work, school, or home. No

6. Continued substance use despite having persistent or recurrent social or interpersonal problem caused or exacerbated by the effects of the substance. Yes

7. Important social, occupational or recreational activities given up or reduced because of substance use. No

8. Recurrent substance use in situations in which it is physically hazardous. Yes

9. Substance use is continued despite knowledge of having a persistent or recurrent physical or psychological problem that is likely to have been caused or exacerbated by the substance. No

10. Tolerance, as defined by either of the following: a. Markedly increased amounts of the substance in order to achieve intoxication or desired effect; b. Markedly diminished effect with continued use of the same amount. Yes

11. Withdrawal, as manifested by either of the following: a. The characteristic withdrawal syndrome for the substance; b. The same (or a closely related) substance is taken to relieve or avoid withdrawal symptoms; Yes

Severity: Severe (6+ symptoms present)

Score 8.0

Behavioral Health Diagnosis for 2019-12-06

Diagnostic Codes	From	Until	Type
F1020 - Alcohol Use Disorder, Severe	2019-12-06		Primary
F4310 - Post-traumatic stress disorder, unspecified	2019-12-06		Secondary
F603 - Borderline personality disorder	2019-12-06		Secondary

Medical Diagnosis for 2019-12-06

Diagnostic Codes

Additional Information for 2019-12-06

Assessment and Plan Patient will be engaged in residential treatment with group therapy, individual counseling, educational sessions, family therapy, and daily Twelve Step groups.

☐ Transfer to Residential Level of Care

Cumberland Heights
8283 River Road Pike
Nashville, TN 37209
EIN: -
Phone: 615-356-2700
Fax: 615-432-3021

Medical - Psychiatric Progress Note

Psychiatric Progress Note for 2019-12-16

Initial Impression: The patient reports continued difficulty with nightmares and triggers. She is also having difficulty with focus and concentration.

She is having difficulty with memory, depression, and increase anxiety.

Mental Status - Appearance: for 2019-12-16

☑ Groomed	☐ Restless	☐ Overly Dramatic
☐ Disheveled	☐ Agitated	☐ Withdrawn
☐ Sickly	☐ Hyperactive	☐ Poor eye contact
☐ Unremarkable	☐ Retarded PMA	☐ Tremors
☐ Fidgety		

Orientation: for 2019-12-16

☑ Time

☑ Person

☑ Place

☑ Situation

Attitude: for 2019-12-16

☑ Cooperative	☐ Arrogant	☐ Guarded
☐ Evasive	☐ Passive-Aggressive	☐ Suspicious
☐ Self-absorbed	☐ Manipulative	☐ Hostile
☐ Passive	☐ Seductive	☐ Intimidating
☐ Hesitant	☐ Demanding	☐ Threatening
☐ Defensive	☐ Antagonistic	

Mood: for 2019-12-16

☐ Euthymic	☑ Anxious	☐ Irritable
☐ Dysphoric	☐ Fearful	☐ Angry
☐ Sad	☐ Despondent	☐ Euphoric
☐ Jovial		

Affect: for 2019-12-16

☑ Depressed	☐ Flat

Cumberland Heights
8283 River Road Pike
Nashville, TN 37209
EIN: -
Phone: 615-356-2700
Fax: 615-432-3021

Clinical - Family Note

Family Session Note for 2019-12-22

Family Present? ⊘ Yes ◯ No

Type: Family Session

Who attended:

Sibling

# of people present: 3

Family Note for 2019-12-22

Family Note Summary: Pt presented for this session with sister on phone. Pt apppeared to be content AEB smiling and expressing looking forward to talking with her sister.

Assessment: Pt expressed the program is good for her and she is planning to follow CCP of sober living for six months. Pt remarked that she has been frustrated with not getting more trauma work done in treatment. Pt appeared to attempt to staff split and focus on that, rather than tx. Counselor challenged her on this, by sharing how the tx team works together to assist her and noting that it is easily to be distracted, and really focus on the day and what she can gain from it. Sister appeared supportive and understanding of pt's past. Sister appeared to regard pt as family and remind her that she is there for her. Pt and sister appeared to have close relationship and awareness of past issues. Pt appeared motivated to follow CCP, stating that she believes she would relapse if she left treatment today. Pt explained triggers being emotional invalidation and anything family related. Pt and sister discussed warning signs that pt is unwell and how to support her in those times. Pt and sister expressed appreciations of one another and session concluded.

Family Note Plan: Pt is recommended to complete inpatient tx and follow through on CCP. Sister is recommended Alanon.

Signatures

12/22/2019 10:35:02 AM

Cumberland Heights
8283 River Road Pike
Nashville, TN 37209
EIN -
Phone: 615-356-2700
Fax: 615-432-3021

Clinical - Individual Note

Individual Note for 2019-12-09

Type: Patient Issue / Concern

Data: Do to earlier thoughts and voiced SI, this writer has been with Pt. one on one for the last hour, and will continue until doctor release her from one on one care. Pt. is stable and engaged in doing her treatment work in the Women's Cabin Community Room

Assessment: Pt. is not in any distress at this time and appea

Plan:

Signatures

███████

_____

███████████████

12/09/2019 11:59:46 AM

Cumberland Heights
8283 River Road Pike
Nashville, TN 37209
EIN: -
Phone: 615-356-2700
Fax: 615-432-3021

Clinical - Individual Note

Individual Note for 2019-12-09

Type: PC Individual Session

Data: This writer met with pt to check-in and complete SRA.

Assessment: Pt presented to session in casual dress and sad mood. Pt reports having thoughts of suicide but no intent. Pt disclosed having a razor in her room that she has been contemplating using. This writer took pt to medical to try and get her moved up to see the doctor today as oppose to tomorrow. This writer took sharp and other potential dangerous objects out of pt's room.

Plan: Pt will begin working on 20 Consequences.

Signatures

████████████████

████████████

12/09/2019 12:52:57 PM

Cumberland Heights
8283 River Road Pike
Nashville, TN 37209
EIN: -
Phone: 615-356-2700
Fax: 615-432-3021

Clinical - Individual Note

Individual Note for 2019-12-11

Type: PC Individual Session

Data: MTP/Step 1 (Pt reports no desired family contact/updates)

This counselor met w/Pony to update her MTP as she transitions to TA from FS. She reported she had already completed her Step 1 assignment so we processed her Step 1 in which she was able to verbalize an understanding of the disease/allergy concept and endorsed total abstinence. We discussed 24hr plan, networking and sponsorship and went into more detail about the disease concept. We processed literature in BB and Basic Text surrounding powerlessness and the solution of self-searching, leveling of pride and confessions of shortcomings as described in literature and how walking out the Steps is more of a process/journey than a checklist.Pony shared her hx of spirituality, being raised as Jehovah's Witness and the loss of her children and family when she chose to disengage herself from this belief system. She reports this traumatic experience happened twice when she again found her children and they refused to re-connect with her. She reports she has tried to practice 12 Step recovery on her own but did not engage in fellowship or sponsorship and we discussed why this was not successful. When we began to process this step, she reported she thought she should be on Step 4, but stated she has a deeper understanding of Step 1 now.

Assessment: Pony seemed alert and oriented. She appeared to struggle with engaging in community and seemed to voice her discomfort w/ Family Programming issues that may trigger her trauma. She ultimately seemed more open to taking suggestions as we worked through Step 1 and seemed more receptive to the process we offer here at CH.

Plan: Continue w/Step 2.

Signatures

12/13/2019 06:53:20 PM

Cumberland Heights
8283 River Road Pike
Nashville, TN 37209
EIN: -
Phone: 615-356-2700
Fax: 615-432-3021

Clinical - Individual Note

Individual Note for 2019-12-17

Type: Spiritual Care Individual

Data: This writer met with Pony for an individual session of pastoral counseling. Pony explained about her upbringing in Jehovah's witness, which she labeled as a cult, and the traumatic experience of leaving this community without her children. Pony shared about getting sober and experienced a 15-month period of sobriety in which she was really active in her church. She talked about temporarily reconnecting with her children at the beginning of this year only to have them cut off contact again. She reports she felt as though talking to them was an answer prayer, and when they cut off contact, she is struggling spiritually to understand why they have been "taken away" from her again. She reports struggling for the past six months with a lot of the "why's" of what she has been through and experienced. This writer talked with Pony about different theological points of view and recognizes that Pony is in a space of exploring theologically what she believes that is different from how she grew up. This writer talked with Pony about the practice of using the Psalms for prayer/meditation and lent her a few books for prayer and a book about the "why's" of suffering.

Assessment: Pony presented as emotionally tired and disconnected

Plan: This writer assigned Pony some theological reading as she works through her experiences of suffering and pain. This writer will follow up with Pony about these readings.

███████████████

Signatures

███████████████

_____

███████████████

12/18/2019 02:43:28 PM

Cumberland Heights
8283 River Road Pike
Nashville, TN 37209
EIN: -
Phone: 615-356-2700
Fax: 615-432-3021

Clinical - Individual Note

Individual Note for 2019-12-18

Type: Clinical Screening Review

Data: This counselor went over screeners w/Pony and conducted SRA due to her having thoughts of harm to self.

Assessment: Pony presented w/flat affect, had appropriate eye contact and shared openly about plan to overdose if she left tx today. She reports she doesn't want to harm herself today and has no plans of leaving tx to complete this plan.

Plan: She will need 24hr f/u.

Signatures

12/18/2019 04:08:05 PM

Cumberland Heights
8283 River Road Pike
Nashville, TN 37209
EIN: -
Phone: 615-356-2700
Fax: 615-432-3021

Clinical - Individual Note

Individual Note for 2019-12-19

Type: Trauma Support

Data: This writer met with ████ "Pony" at the request of her PC. She stated that she is still living her trauma. She shared that she got out of a cult and had her children taken from her about 5 years ago. Earlier this year, she attempted to visit her children in California and they refused to come, which she reported brought everything back and caused her to be suicidal. She reported she has done some EMDR sessions and they helped, but she stopped seeing her therapist after the failed visit with kids.

Assessment: Pony presented at depressed, tearful at times. She stated she struggles with seeing the point in living. She was willing to accept suggestions.

Plan: Pony was given a some templates for a gratitude journal to complete daily. She was also encouraged to continue EMDR with therapist after D/C, as well as DBT skills group and individual therapy.

Signatures

████████████████

████████████████

12/19/2019 12:02:34 PM

Cumberland Heights
8283 River Road Pike
Nashville, TN 37209
EIN -
Phone: 615-356-2700
Fax: 615-432-3021

Clinical - Individual Note

Individual Note for 2019-12-20

Type: Patient Issue / Concern

Data: This writer met with patient to complete CSSR ████ CSSR screening required 24 hour follow up. This writer notified Lead Counselor ████ and Clinical Director ████ to determine what best course of action to take as patient as reported SI to the degree that requires 24 hour CSSR.

Assessment: This writer felt that consistently completing CSSR without addressing the reasoning for the CSSR, and also patient appears to be desensitized to the assessment tool as she was giving prompts as to which numbers this writer needed to select during the assessment.

Plan: Patient will be seen by medical for SI evaluation. Patient will meet with this writer over the weekend and check in, instead of us asking the same CSSR questions she already answered time after time unless her SI increases to which we will then complete CSSR. Quality management was notified and help develop this plan. Patients primary counselor will take over in meeting with patient on Monday for check ins and we can re-visit plan on Monday in morning meeting and amend if needed.

Signatures

12/20/2019 11:51:34 AM

Cumberland Heights
8283 River Road Pike
Nashville, TN 37209
EIN: -
Phone: 615-356-2700
Fax: 615-432-3021

Clinical - Individual Note

Individual Note for 2019-12-21

Type: Patient Issue / Concern

Data: This writer met with pt to address pts previous CSSR that required 24 hour follow up. Patient verbalized her frustration with her clinical needs and how she feels they are not being addressed. This writer reviewed all noted individual sessions with pt to determine where any clinical needs were lacking. Pt identified having multiple individual sessions with various clinical staff, however stated those sessions were very surface and she felt as she was being "lost in the shuffle". This writer informed pt that she would notify clinical staff of pts frustrations. Pt stated that she has no thoughts of harming or killing herself. Pt stated " I actually dont want to die today. I believe I am feeling somewhat better". Pt verbalized feeling hopeful and requested that this writer contact clinical staff with patients concerns about her thoughts of receiving less than optimal clinical treatment. This writer assured pt that clinical staff is committed to giving her the most evidence based practices to address addiction and will continue to notify appropriate staff of pts view in regard to her clinical experience.

Assessment: Pt presented AAOx4. Pt verbalized having no SI/HI or thoughts of harming herself. Pt stated that she has had no thoughts of wishing she were dead. Pt continued to blame clinical staff for her feeling "not well and not doing anything to get well". Pt was adamant that she has been fully engaged in her treatment and believes that clinical staff is lacking in effectiveness.

Plan: This writer will notify clinical treatment team of pts frustrations with her clinical experience.

Signatures

12/21/2019 05:18:47 PM

Cumberland Heights
8283 River Road Pike
Nashville, TN 37209
EIN: ·
Phone: 615-356-2700
Fax: 615-432-3021

Clinical - Individual Note

Individual Note for 2019-12-22

Type: General

Data: This writer met with ███████ " Pony" to assess her SI as was previous planned by tx team due to her consistent CSSR ratings that required 24 hour follow ups.

Assessment: ███████ stated that she has minimal depression and no longer has any thoughts of wishing she was dead. ███████ stated " I am finally getting more clear minded about what I need to do to get better and overcome my depression.". ███████ stated that she does not feel she is getting any clinical work completed due to staff not addressing her grief and loss. ███████ stated that she believes that her clinical team have been "wasting time" by having her repeat her story and not addressing her grief and lose. This writer sent email to spiritual staff who also do grief/loss work with patients, so that an individual session could be completed. ███████ continued to complain about all her clinical sessions. ███████ stated that she believes clinical staff have avoided contacting her previous therapist to develop a collaborative treatment plan. This writer informed ███████ that an email will be sent to PC to request contact be made with previous counselor to develop a plan that also included ███████ in the redevelopment of clinical goals that was first established.

Plan: This writer will notify ███████ PC to request contact with pts past therapist.

Signatures

12/22/2019 09:19:48 PM

Cumberland Heights
8283 River Road Pike
Nashville, TN 37209
EIN: -
Phone: 615-356-2700
Fax: 615-432-3021

Clinical - Individual Note

Individual Note for 2019-12-24

Type: PC Individual Session

Data: Step 3

This counselor met w/Pony ███████ to process her Step 3 assignment, which was well thought out and complete. She verbalized an understanding of self-will and a desire to seek guidance from HP. She was able to identify self pity and changing old ideas. She had difficulty identifying self will since being in tx and attempted to connect our present work w/issues over the weekend w/weekend Supervisor. This was easily redirected and she was ultimately able to identify areas that she believes is using her voice, but has difficulty knowing when to use her voice and when to surrender. We discussed have the ability to identify when she has reached that place and allowing HP to set the limits of her using her voice to advocate for herself and when it turns into self will run riot. We then processed how she identified using concept of Step 10 and how surrendering the fight for her right to meet w/her children brings peace instead of generating the depression when she continues to fight the injustices having to be separated from them and experience the loss. We also discussed that she identifies working Step 3 concept as she was not accepted into sober living that she applied for and that CH is limited in the way in which she feel she should be addressing her grief more.

Assessment: It appears there has been some progress as she has identified that the main complaint she has as far as what she has gotten from CH is that she feels her grief has not been addressed, although she has had several individual appointments w/other therapists such as Trauma Therapist, Pastoral Counselors, Art Therapist. She seems to recognize that her medications have stabilized and she is not feeling SI/HI or having thoughts of harm to self or others. She appears to connect this to use of the concepts of the Steps in tx.

Plan: This counselor is still unsure if Pony will be leaving for Sober Living prior to her scheduled DC date so she received a written form of identifying concept of Steps 4-5 until she is secure in her CCP.

Signatures

12/24/2019 11:51:21 AM

Cumberland Heights
8283 River Road Pike
Nashville, TN 37209
EIN: -
Phone: 615-356-2700
Fax: 615-432-3021

Clinical - CM / CCP Note

Case Management / Continuing Care Plan Note for 2019-12-27

Type CM / CCP Meeting

CM / CCP Note Summary: Pt presented to writer's office and indicated that she did not intend to go to sober-living and that she has made the decision to go to Palm Springs, CA to live with her best friend. Pt states that she wants to reconnect with her children and says, "I know I am going to have to face it some time. I came to Nashville to run away from the pain but now it is time for me to try." Writer discussed the importance of developing positive recover support as going back to the area where her family lives could be potentially very triggering. Writer asked pt if she has considered that her children may not be ready to connect yet and that additional time in sober-living could help prepare her for whatever outcome she might face. Pt states that she has support from her friends in the area and is open to IOP. Pt signed and ROI for Hazeldon in the Rancho Mirage area and writer/pt called to find out about IOP. Pt asked what would happen if she lost her insurance due to having to quite her job here in Nashville and was informed by Hazeldon that she would not be able to participate in their IOP. Pt states that she will go back to her roommate's house here in Nashville for "a couple of days" and sell everything that she can. Pt reports that she will then drive to California.

CM / CCP Note Plan: Writer will follow-up with Treatment Team regarding pt's discharge plan. Writer will consult with Business Development staff to see if there are approved, grant-funded facilities for IOP in pt's area.

Safe Start for 2019-12-27

Discussed the following topics and the patient stated understanding:

    Extended Release Naltrexone Injections

    Patient agrees to Vivitrol injections? ○ Yes ⊘ No

Comments: Pt continues to decline

Aftercare Attendance for 2019-12-27

Aftercare Attendance this week? N/A

If "No", Why?

Signatures

12/27/2019 06:44:07 PM

Cumberland Heights
8283 River Road Pike
Nashville, TN 37209
EIN: -
Phone: 615-356-2700
Fax: 615-432-3021

Clinical - CM / CCP Note

Case Management / Continuing Care Plan Note for 2020-01-02

Type Final CCP Meeting

CM / CCP Note Summary: Patient is ready to discharge today. CCP has been reviewed with patient who states understanding and agreement with CCP. Pt denies signs or symptoms of withdrawal. Pt also denies SI or HI. Current affect is appropriate; mood is congruent. About leaving treatment, pt states "I feel good, excited, ready to go home and get my life together." Information about the potential for overdose after a period of abstinence, the emergency use of Narcan for reversal of opioid overdose, and the use of Vivitrol injections to support early recovery was reviewed again and patient states understanding. She continues to refuse Vivitrol injections as part of CCP, but is aware that she can contact this writer if she changes her mind. Pt states her immediate recovery plans are to "go to a meeting. There is one right down the street from my house." Pt has completed her Patient Satisfaction Survey. A copy of her Fire Drill Plan, a Recovery Contact, Presence in Treatment letter, AA/ NA Meeting List and a Return to Work Letter were included in her Discharge Package. A copy of the Return to Work Letter and Presence in Treatment Letter were sent to medical records for scanning to pt chart. She will be discharging and driving herself around 10:00am. Routing information given.

CM / CCP Note Plan: Discharge complete.

Safe Start for 2020-01-02

Discussed the following topics and the patient stated understanding.

Tolerance

Increased Overdose Risk Following Abstinence

ER Use of Narcan for Reversal of Opioid OD

Extended Release Naltrexone Injections

Patient agrees to Vivitrol injections? ◯ Yes ⊘ No

Comments: Declines but is aware that she can call this writer to schedule if she changes her mind.

Aftercare Attendance for 2020-01-02

Aftercare Attendance this week? N/A

If "No", Why?

Signatures

01/02/2020 09:27:24 AM

Cumberland Heights
8283 River Road Pike
Nashville, TN 37209
EIN: -
Phone: 615-356-2700
Fax: 615-432-3021

Clinical - Group Notes

Group Note for 2019-12-23

Session Date 2019-12-23

Started 14:30

Ended 15:15

Group Title Specialty: Trauma Care/PTSI

Group Description This writer met with ██████ to administer a trauma screen. She did not disclose the source of possible trauma.

Group Documentation Instructions for 2019-12-23

Psycho-education Group

Please complete only the Data: Engagement Section if any of the above groups are selected.

Please complete all sections below if Group Counseling is selected.

Data: Engagement for 2019-12-23

Attentive

Gave Feedback

Comments: The following are the trauma scores:
15 Trauma Shame: Feeling unworthy and having self-hate because of trauma experience.
13 Trauma Bonding: Being connected (loyal, helpful, supportive) to people who are dangerous, shaming, or exploitive.
8 Trauma Blocking: A pattern exists to numb, block out, or overwhelm feelings that stem from trauma in your life.
7 Trauma Reactions: Experiencing current reactions to trauma events in the past.
6 Trauma Repetition: Repeating behaviors or situations which parallel early trauma experiences.
5 Trauma Splitting: Ignoring traumatic realities by dissociating or "splitting off" experience parts of self.
4 Trauma Abstinence: Depriving yourself of things you need or deserve because of traumatic acts.
1 Trauma Pleasure: Finding pleasure in the presence of danger, violence, risk, or shame.
Scores 0 to 3 are low and not an area of concern. Scores 3 to 6 are moderate and an area to discuss with therapist. Above 6 is high and is an area in need of intense focus. Based on this screening, Pony

Cumberland Heights
8283 River Road Pike
Nashville, TN 37209
EIN: -
Phone: 615-356-2700
Fax: 615-432-3021

would benefit from EMDR around her trauma. She will be referred to
an EMDR therapist upon discharge.

Specify Other:

Data: Affect for 2019-12-23

Comments: Specify Other:

Data: Mood for 2019-12-23

Specify Other:

Pt Reported Rating of Depression: Comments:

Pt Reported Rating of Anxiety:

Pt Reported Rating of Irritability:

Data: Thought Content / Process for 2019-12-23

Specify Other:

Comments

Data: Behaviors for 2019-12-23

Comments: Specify Other:

Reported Physical Symptoms for 2019-12-23

Pt Reported Rating of Craving:

Progress for 2019-12-23

Progress made toward goal? ○ Yes ○ No

Comments:

Pt Reported Triggers/Obstacles:

Pt Reported Recovery Skills Practice:

Clinical Impressions for 2019-12-23

Assessment:

Plan:

Cumberland Heights
8283 River Road Pike
Nashville, TN 37209
EIN: -
Phone: 615-356-2700
Fax: 615-432-3021

Assessments - Trauma Screening

LEC-5 for 2019-12-08

Listed below are a number of difficult or stressful things that sometimes happen to people. For each event check one or more of the boxes to the right to indicate that: (a) it happened to you personally; (b) you witnessed it happen to someone else; (c) you learned about it happening to a close family member or close friend; (d) you were exposed to it as part of your job (for example, paramedic, police, military, or other first responder); (e) you're not sure if it fits, or (f) it doesn't apply to you.

Be sure to consider your entire life (growing up as well as adulthood) as you go through the list of events.

Event	Happened To Me	Witnessed It	Learned About It	Part Of My Job	Not Sure	Doesn't Apply
1. Natural disaster (for example, flood, hurricane, tornado, earthquake)	☑	☐	☐	☐	☐	☐
2. Fire or explosion	☐	☐	☐	☐	☐	☑
3. Transportation accident (for example, car accident, boat accident, train wreck, plane crash)	☐	☑	☐	☐	☐	☐
4. Serious accident at work, home, or during recreational activity	☐	☑	☐	☐	☐	☐
5. Exposure to toxic substance (for example, dangerous chemicals, radiation)	☐	☐	☐	☐	☐	☑
6. Physical assault (for example, being attacked, hit, slapped, kicked, beaten up)	☑	☐	☐	☐	☐	☐
7. Assault with a weapon (for example, being shot, stabbed, threatened with a knife, gun, bomb)	☐	☐	☐	☐	☐	☑
8. Sexual assault (rape, attempted rape, made to	☑	☐	☐	☐	☐	☐

Cumberland Heights
8283 River Road Pike
Nashville, TN 37209
EIN: -
Phone: 615-356-2700
Fax: 615-432-3021

perform any type of sexual act through force or threat of harm)					
9. Other unwanted or uncomfortable sexual experience	☑	☐	☐	☐	☐	☐
10. Combat or exposure to a war-zone (in the military or as a civilian)	☐	☐	☑	☐	☐	☐
11. Captivity (for example, being kidnapped, abducted, held hostage, prisoner of war)	☐	☐	☐	☐	☐	☑
12. Life-threatening illness or injury	☐	☑	☐	☐	☐	☐
13. Severe human suffering	☐	☑	☐	☐	☐	☐
14. Sudden violent death (for example, homicide, suicide)	☐	☐	☑	☐	☐	☐
15. Sudden accidental death	☐	☐	☑	☐	☐	☐
16. Serious injury, harm, or death you caused to someone else	☐	☐	☐	☐	☐	☑
17. Any other very stressful event or experience	☑	☐	☐	☐	☐	☐

PCL-5 for 2019-12-08

Below is a list of problems that people sometimes have in response to a very stressful experience. Please read each problem carefully and then select one of the numbers to the right to indicate how much you have been bothered by that problem in the past month.

1. Repeated, disturbing, and unwanted memories of the stressful experience? 4 = Extremely

2. Repeated, disturbing dreams of the stressful experience? 4 = Extremely

3. Suddenly feeling or acting as if the stressful experience were actually happening again (as if you were actually back there reliving it)? 4 = Extremely

4. Feeling very upset when something reminded you of the stressful experience?of a stressful experience from the past? 4 = Extremely

Cumberland Heights
3283 River Road Pike
Nashville, TN 37209
EIN: -
Phone: 615-356-2700
Fax: 615-432-3021

5. Having strong physical reactions when something reminded you of the stressful experience (for example, heart pounding, trouble breathing, sweating)? 4 = Extremely

6. Avoiding memories, thoughts, or feelings related to the stressful experience? 4 = Extremely

7. Avoiding external reminders of the stressful experience (for example, people, places, conversations, activities, objects, or situations)? 4 = Extremely

8. Trouble remembering important parts of the stressful experience? 4 = Extremely

9. Having strong negative beliefs about yourself, other people, or the world (for example, having thoughts such as: I am bad, there is something seriously wrong with me, no one can be trusted, the world is completely dangerous)? 4 = Extremely

10. Blaming yourself or someone else for the stressful experience or what happened after it? 4 = Extremely

11. Having strong negative feelings such as fear, horror, anger, guilt, or shame?have loving feelings for those close to you? 4 = Extremely

12. Loss of interest in activities that you used to enjoy? 3 = Quite a bit

13. Feeling distant or cut off from other people? 4 = Extremely

14. Trouble experiencing positive feelings (for example, being unable to feel happiness or have loving feelings for people close to you)? 3 = Quite a bit

15. Irritable behavior, angry outbursts, or acting aggressively? 1 = A little bit

16. Taking too many risks or doing things that could cause you harm? 1 = A little bit

17. Being "superalert" or watchful or on guard? 4 = Extremely

18. Feeling jumpy or easily startled? 2 = Moderately

19. Having difficulty concentrating? 4 = Extremely

20. Trouble falling or staying asleep? 2 = Moderately

Score 68.0

Summing all 20 items (range 0-80) all scores totally 33 or higher refer to trauma care groups.

Assessment Results and Recommendations for 2019-12-08

Assessment Results: ██████ verbalizes " I have had a lifetime of trauma" ██████ verbalizes her cult was a life complex PTSD. ██████ has a history of trauma work to begin healing her trauma, however 2 weeks ago attempted suicide because she found her children on social media and scheduled a meet up with them. When she arrived at the scheduled meeting her children refused contact and dropped all forms of contact including social media ██████ then attempted suicide 5 months later on her daughter birthday.

Refer to trauma care groups? ⊘ Yes ○ No

Explain:

This writer is referring ██████ to trauma groups: individual sessions as ██████ recently attempted suicide (11/20/2019) as result of having triggered past traumas due to her children refusing to have contact with her. ██████ will benefit for trauma grounding to utilize in times of traumatic responses.

Signatures